W9-CZH-582

LET'S CELEBRATE PET BIRDS

PET BIRD CARE

T.J. LAFEBER, D.V.M.

Lafeber Company

Odell, IL 60460

Revised edition copyright 1989
LAFEBER CO. T.J. LAFEBER, D.V.M.
Previous title Tender Loving Care for Pet Birds
Copyright 1977, T.J. LAFEBER, D.V.M.
Original Edition 1977
3rd printing 1983

Library of Congress Number 89-084266
ISBN 0-960526-2-8

Illustrated by: Ruth Lenover
Leslie De Courcey

MOST PEOPLE LIKE BIRDS

AND,
MOST BIRDS DELIGHT
IN BECOMING THE FRIENDS
OF PEOPLE.

TABLE OF CONTENTS

1 THE VALUE OF PET BIRDS

Popularity

Birds have finally come to the forefront as truly desirable companion animals. It has taken a long time but more people now enjoy birds as pets than ever before. Their popularity has increased not only in the United States, but throughout the world.

In the U.S. approximately 15 million birds reside in homes as pets. The exact numbers are impossible to determine, but considering the numbers of birds raised in this country and the numbers imported year after year, the estimate of 15 million seems conservative. Some authorities claim twice that number are in homes.

Not just a recent fad, this growth has been slow but steady since 1960. The trend will continue as more and more people realize all the wonderful qualities of these spectacular animals.

Changing life styles—more women working, city living, mobile society, ease of care in a fast-paced world—have been suggested as reasons for the high popularity of birds as pets. These explanations are certainly valid, but by no means express the whole picture.

The reason birds are popular is simply because they can become excellent pets.

If birds were not extremely fascinating and lovable, they would never have charmed so many people.

Birds give much and ask little in return.

1

Friendship

Advantages of Pet Birds	Rating
Friendly	A
Affectionate	A
Communicative	A
Economical	A
Beautiful	A
Long-lived	A
Easily cared for	A
Convenient	A
Entertaining	A
Recreational	A

Birds Become Our Friends

Birds are eager to be our friends, but resist friendship until they can trust us. This is quite different from puppies who immediately seek our attention and affection. Figuratively speaking, the shoe is on the other foot when it comes to birds. We must prove our consistent friendliness, caring attitude, and overall goodness before birds accept and trust us.

When we have built TRUST and have become a friend, birds want:

> to be near us
>
> to be a companion that shares activities
>
> to sit on our hand, arm or shoulder
>
> to eat out of our hand
>
> to perform for us by doing tricks
>
> to talk or sing or "show off" in some manner

Birds learn to trust us.

Birds have the ability to live in harmony with people, and, in fact, can learn to love their owners. They want our attention and companionship. In homes they would like to become part of the family.

The love and trust displayed by pet birds may be their greatest contribution to people. Birds adapt well to people of all ages and to most circumstances placed upon them by their owners. This versatility allows birds to be with children or adults equally well and to live in

3

close or spacious conditions. What other animal could live happily for years with shut-ins, in nursing and retirement homes or even in prison cells?

**Your bird wants to be your FRIEND.
Help him to become a loving pet.**

Yes, these little animals have much to offer those who understand and love them.

> People like these qualities of pet birds:
>
> sociability
>
> friendliness
>
> bright and spirited manners
>
> happy attitude
>
> curious and playful nature
>
> vocalization (talking and singing)

Brings Nature Into Your Lives

From the dawn of civilization, birds have been deeply involved in our lives.

How could birds not be involved with the development of mankind when they have been constantly part of our surroundings? That birds have had a role in religious worship, art, decoration, ceremonies, symbols, sports, hunting, engineering and history is not surprising. No other wild animals have made their presence more obvious, both physically and vocally.

A myriad of reasons exist as to why people like pets so much. But beyond obvious explanations are there deeper reasons?

Perhaps, we feel comfortable and relaxed with pets because of some innate or hereditary factor. Our forefathers spent their lives involved with animals. Tending livestock and working with animals is ingrained into our lives. Not even a hundred years ago, most of our relatives were still in agriculture. Today many people relax when walking their dog, petting their cat, working in their gardens, or with plants in their homes. Being city people now does not mean that our heritage of agriculture has left us. In fact, our background obviously shows itself as you watch the multitudes of city people enjoying their animals and plants.

Evidently, we still have cravings for those things in nature that were so vital for millions of years. Pets may be satisfying this inner need.

> Pets lend a tranquility and peacefulness to our lives not possible from commercial entertainment.

<u>Birds help bring nature into our lives and homes.</u>

Entertainment and Recreation

Whether a person wants relaxation, amusement or entertainment, birds will supply hours, days and even years of pleasure. As far as being enjoyable pets, birds fulfill the requirements as well as any other animal. Many owners find interesting challenges in taming and training birds or in raising them (aviculture).

Proud companions

Helps Overcome Loneliness

Inanimate objects might temporarily entertain a lonely person, but it takes a living animal with emotions and sensitivities to fill a void. The hole in the heart of a lonely person can only be helped when filled with love and attention from another living animal. Possibly one of the best alternatives for such a person, then, is a bird.

An excellent way to help lonely people would be to give them a hand tamed parakeet or a hand-raised baby bird. These birds have the friendliness of a puppy from the beginning. Ask your pet store owner!

6

One of the Least Understood Pets

Although one encounters birds daily, an aura of puzzle and mystery surrounds them. No other wild animal exposes himself as much, whether in the city or country, by the coast or inland, in North or South; and yet most people only know them by their colorful feathers, free spirits and bright song. Birds allow people to know them only superficially and hide their true identities. They make nests in limbs of trees above our yards, in mail boxes and garages. So close to us and yet so far.

We think of birds as fragile creatures and don't often consider they survive the long, cold winter or return in the spring after a 2,000 mile migration.

How many people know that a bird can be a friend?

How many people know that birds are an animal of many emotions?

How many people know that if birds get sick they can be treated as effectively as dogs and cats?

The simple truth is that while many people are educated about wild birds, not many people know much about pet birds.

I hope after reading this book you will regard birds as loving and exciting pets.

Birds Can Contribute to the Greater Community

Concerned parents may use birds as an acceptable method of motivating their children and teaching responsibility.

Teachers use pet birds in classroom situations to add excitement and interest.

Pet birds are an advantage when used in rehabilitation programs for people who are physically handicapped, mentally disturbed, retarded, hospitalized, or confined to nursing homes or correctional facilities.

The joy that birds bring to these people's lives is heart warming.

Pride of Ownership

Would you be proud—
    to associate with a World
    Class Super Athlete?

    to have one of the
    "Greatest Wonders of the
    World" in your home?

    to possess a creature of
    unmatched beauty?

    to be able to show your
    friends the glories of a
    bird?

    to be responsible for the
    care and welfare of a bird?

    to share the happiness that
    birds radiate?

    to introduce others to the
    fun of owning a bird?

One of the "Greatest Wonders of the World."

There is no doubt that a person can take real pride in being an owner of one of nature's greatest achievements—birds.

Bird Care is Relatively Easy, Inexpensive and Convenient

Because of a bird's size and basic requirements, the average person will not be overburdened with even the ultimate in bird care.

Changing cage papers, supplying fresh water, and feeding are the chores of bird care and can be performed quickly. Hand feeding, taming and training involve more time, but usually fit in well with personal daily routines.

How expensive can feeding a pet bird be? A canary eats one teaspoon of food daily, and a large parrot eats up to two ounces of food. So the cost of food is minimal.

Economical

When traveling, your bird goes with you easily in the car or in a plane. The large cage won't be needed,—only a small carrier. Or if it's just a week-end trip—plan to leave the bird home with extra food and water, and someone to "look in".

If it happens that you don't get the cage paper changed for a day or two, it is acceptable. Bird droppings are odorless, so your guests will not be offended. Normally, birds are odorless; but if they do smell, check with your veterinarian, or maybe they simply need a cleansing bath.

Further, birds offer the advantage of never having to be taken out of the home for exercise. However, on a nice day they will enjoy the "out of doors" freshness just as you do. Of course, they either have to be in a cage or "grounded" by having their flight feathers cut.

Overcoming Fear of Animals

The fear that some children have of animals and birds can be lessened by having a parakeet sit on their finger and eat out of their hand.

Even adults' fear has been eased by the friendliness of little parakeets or other small birds.

Pet Birds Can Bring Unexpected Happiness

The happy, little surprises of life bring people much joy. No one would ordinarily suspect that a little bird could bring some people so much fun. Pet birds can become one of the unanticipated, pleasant happenings, and sometimes it's the most unexpected person that becomes enchanted by birds.

Birds return love for a little food and kindness. Even the work of caring for them turns into a reward for being considerate.

"Feel the love a bird can give."

Birds don't "ring the bell" for everyone, but when they do, it's exciting.

The "power of friendship" is impressive even if it's from one of nature's smallest creatures.

One of the Hardiest of the World's Creatures

You may never have considered that birds are world class super athletes. Daily they perform aerial feats impossible for other vertebrates. Soaring, diving, take-offs and landings look easy and yet show power and strength. Flying high over mountains, crossing lakes, oceans and deserts, migrating for hundreds or thousands of miles, illustrates birds' stamina and hardiness, and probably makes them the Greatest Wonder of the World.

The World's Foremost Super Athlete

Their hardiness goes even further. Birds regularly survive hardship and sickness often better than other animals that have a reputation for being tough.

Longevity speaks for itself. The life expectancy of most small birds is roughly ten years; medium size birds live fifteen to twenty-five years, and larger members of the parrot family survive for twenty-five to sixty years.

When fed balanced diets, taken to veterinarians for check-ups and given reasonable care, birds live long, productive lives. Veterinarians will tell you that birds are good patients, and like cats—have nine lives.

11

2 BIRDS CAN BECOME VALUABLE PETS

Life in the Wild

Because of the multiple advantages for birds, nature's prescription for survival in the wild included living in a flock. "Congregation-living" has become part of their make-up. Except for a few instances birds rarely lead a solitary life.

Living closely together requires adjusting and accepting all the other members of the group. Turmoil and strife would destroy the flock. Thus, flocks have need for a highly disciplined social structure that mandates a life of harmony. But how do they maintain law and order? What sort of system do they have for keeping peace without an army or police force?

Their method of discipline is excellent. Each bird involves himself in a system of controls—and each bird knows his place and the place of all the others in the flock. If anyone steps out of line, all the members know it and are upset about it. It's either do right or get out of the flock.

This achievement could not have been accomplished without their friendly nature and calm submission to others. They have learned to accept their place in a group without hostility or thoughts of revenge. Birds are "team players" and know how to get along with the others in their group.

Nature has made birds social animals not too different in many ways from humans. Compare these social requirements to your own.

Getting along well with others comes natural to birds.

They need companionship and do the best when living as a friend of everyone.

They require an untroubled life—no stress, no fear and no anxiety. To be at their peak, they need to be content.

Security and safety are always uppermost in their mind. The presence of friendly people and a proper environment provide this.

Birds cuddle; like to touch and be touched; want to be petted, scratched and rubbed; desire to sit on your finger, hands, arms, shoulders; and like to share with us when we eat and drink.

Part of being a social animal means participating in communications—to verbalize and receive a response.

13

Birds' way of life in the wild has prepared them well for living in captivity as companions to people.

Their temperament and behavior have been mellowed through the necessity of being a "right guy" in the flock. As a result the steps from living as a wild animal to becoming a tame, loving pet are small.

Being a "right guy" in the wild prepares birds to be good pets.

Birds Can Become Valuable Pets

Do you understand why millions of birds worldwide have become successful pets in homes? What has initiated the increased interest in birds over the last 25 years? Have birds changed and suddenly become a desirable animal, or have people just recognized their attributes?

These seem to be pertinent questions for bird owners. Another question and maybe of equal concern—Can birds be as happy in homes as they would have been in the wild?

The answer to all these questions hinges upon the mentality of birds—their personality, emotions, and ability to learn and to adjust.

In general, nature seems to have designed birds to live equally well both in the wild and in homes as pets! Their heritage prepares them well for relating to people and being domesticated. This has been proven repeatedly by the millions of successful birds in homes.

Their qualities of fun and friendship, their desire to talk, sing, perform, play, and to be a companion endears them to man. However, all these attributes would mean nothing if birds could not adjust to living with people.

Bringing birds into home situations which prohibit free flight would seem to go against what nature has instilled into birds over millions of years. And yet, birds show no behavioral or psychological effects from being denied flight.

So successfully have birds adapted themselves to life in the wild that numerically they outnumber all the other land vertebrates. There are approximately 8700 living species of birds as compared with 3000 amphibians, 6000 reptiles, and 4100 mammals.

Could it be that the adaptability of birds will allow them to accomplish in captivity what they have done in the wild?

Yes, that same ability has allowed them to become pets in millions of homes worldwide. If the trend continues, birds could eventually outnumber cats and dogs as pets.

Some day birds will be the most popular pet.

How much difference is there between a wild and a tame bird? Maybe not so much!!

Communication

Birds might well be described as gregarious social animals.

Birds communicate more messages and have larger vocabularies than any other animal except humans. By comparison, other animals are a quiet lot.

This song is dedicated to his owner.

Birds' spirited activities and colorful feathers set the stage, but nothing adds to the scene more than their vocalizations. In fact, birds might be considered the song and dance act of the animal world. It's difficult to think of a bird without including singing or calling. Birds like to express themselves and do an excellent job of it.

15

At times birds can be heard babbling away seemingly expressing views on many subjects, as if explaining to everyone their ideas on life.

Why did nature allow birds to become so noisy? Should you talk to your parrot, or whistle to your canary? (Of course! They're talking to you.)

If shunned or avoided, birds suffer from loneliness.

Ordinarily, silence is golden for survival in the wild, and only broken at certain times. Nature allows birds to be an exception to the rule.

Perhaps talking, singing or chirping convey a bird's feelings just as much as laughing and crying does for a person. Expression seems to be important. They want to communicate. Sometimes these utterances broadcast messages to be heard. At other times they seem to vocalize for their own benefit. Regardless, the development of their respiratory system allows for a wide range of precise modulated and highly complex sounds which gives the power to express happiness, joy, satisfaction and sadness. Interestingly, they seem to acquire more power with use.

Vocal communication needs to be shared, and birds do this well. They hear and respond—sometimes in sound and sometimes with actions. Why not? An important part of their life is being social. They want companionship and communication is part of being a friend. When someone listens to them and answers or acknowledges them, they're delighted. It's lonely talking in an empty room or when no one is listening, but exciting when another living thing responds freely with positive feedback.

Birds want to be heard.

In pet birds' song, talking or chattering, they seem to say:

Hello, I'm happy to see you.

Let me out of my cage.

Scratch my head.

I love you.

I'm hungry.

It's time for bed.

Please talk to me.

Learning Ability and Performance

Learning ability has helped birds become one of the most successful wild animals, and is an important key to birds becoming excellent pets.

Owners of birds may be fascinated to learn that those physical talents so admired in the wild, are only part of birds' capabilities. The other part—personality, emotions, behavior, attitude—has to do with their minds. Birds are smart animals. (This conflicts with the insulting remark in which someone might be referred to as a "bird brain".)

Maybe in the past birds have been considered to be of low intellect since their brain is tiny and noteably backward in development of the cerebral cortex.

More talent than might be imagined.

17

However, "birds have demonstrated in test after test that they are capable of highly intelligent behavior, sometimes surpassing the abilities of mammals with greatly superior cortical development."*

Observing birds' behavior in the wild forecasts their attitude and actions in captivity.

Learning starts for the baby bird before he leaves the nest. Even the short period living in a nest with other babies teaches a type of community living. Also, small nests forces close living with other birds, which means learning rules of behavior.

School is short. Birds must learn from their parents quickly. Within two weeks after being hatched baby robins will leave their nests—not much time until they graduate to test their knowledge in the wild. After that, it's learn from good and bad experiences, trial and error and association with other birds. Sometimes there is no second chance.

Birds in homes learn to trust people and to live and enjoy life in captivity.

BIRDS CAN LOVE THEIR OWNERS
This is one of the most important aspects of bird ownership.

Emotion—The Key to Birds Being Companion Animals

How much friendship, campanionship or affection can be expected from pet birds?

What we're really interested in is determining birds' emotional capacity.

Birds demonstrate happiness, fear, aggression, jealousy, appeasement, defensiveness, nervousness and loneliness.

Most importantly birds can love people. Radiating from this affection comes the desire to perform, entertain and relate to their owners. Thus they sing, talk, mimic, dance, play, do tricks and display.

The next time you approach a frightened, nervous, hostile bird—possibly angry—remember that the pendulum of emotions swings in both directions. They have feelings just as strong in the opposite direction. A bird that shows anger can have just as an intense love. Unpleasant characteristics can be surpassed by pleasant ones.

All of these emotions can be observed in birds:

Love

Joy

Sadness

Fear

Anger

Indifference

Love

Birds never tell us about their feelings...or do they?
What type of feelings would you say these acts describe?
Birds:

Eagerly anticipate your arrival and when you
enter the room are excited to see you.

Want to be with you.

Mimic your voice because
they try to imitate their
owner

Move close to you, cuddle
and want to be touched.

Look forward to sharing
your food.

Good Pals

Joyfully perform tricks
and try to entertain you.

Trust you. (That's saying a lot because in trusting you completely their lives could be at stake.)

Put their heads down submissively to be scratched.

Take pleasure in communicating with you through sounds and body language.

Call for your attention.

Have a feeling that they have become members of our family.

May become jealous and even attack whomever they consider a competitor.

Become so attached to you that in your prolonged absence may feel stressed, depressed or even psychotic. (May start feather picking and manifest other nervous vices.)

Sit contentedly on your hand or shoulder.

Need your friendship and attention to be happy.

> With this type of devotion toward humans, I think it is fair to conclude that birds can love us.

Joy

Birds seem to epitomize joy and happiness more than any other animal.

Singing, whistling, lively talking, dancing, spirited activities and friendship represent joy and happiness in the lives of people. Birds characteristically do all these things and so we understand them to be happy animals.

Birds, seem to continuously vocalize that they are doing fine—life is good to them and meant to be enjoyed.

"Whoppee" Given the opportunity pet birds show their happy ways.

Many birds' activities seem to be playful pursuits, and play is almost synonymous with fun and joy. While young birds learn much about their environment and improve their skills through play, adult birds continue the playful habits of youth and enlarge them to include many more games and tricks. Both play and learning continue as long as they live.

Loneliness

Try to place yourself in a pet bird's shoes, and it may then occur to you that some pet birds lead solitary lives. Loneliness can't be detected from the expression on their faces, but, nonetheless, it takes a toll internally.

Birds resemble humans in that they are social animals that live within a group of animals. Most of their activites in the wild are with members of their species. Being in captivity doesn't change their inherent need to have a social life.

Birds living a life of isolation do poorly.

Fortunately, pet birds can be brought into our society, and can be our companions.

> Pet birds need people.

Fear—The Culprit

Understandably, most people like birds. And most birds would like people too, if fear didn't get in the way.

Why is fear such an important factor in birds?

Fear of animals (including people) has been ingrained into birds. At birth birds instinctively know that all animals might be dangerous predators and to fear them.

Birds in the wild have an almost perfect answer to every threatening situation. As soon as their "early warning system" detects anything strange, they immediately take flight to an inaccessible height or to a

21

At first, birds see people as dangerous predators—to be feared and avoided.

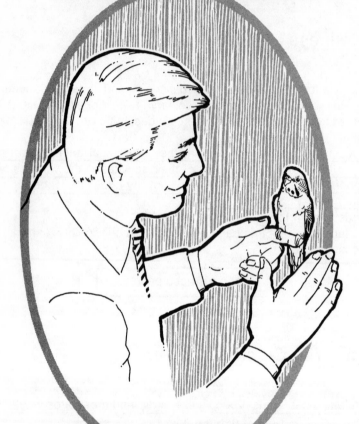

Remove fear **and birds become loving pets, eager to live happily in our homes.**

place where they can hide. Flight is the answer to every problem that involves fear.

So successful has been escape by flight that birds never had to develop any other answer. Not that birds had much choice. Obviously, they are not fighters—their lightweight, delicate bodies could not withstand any kind of blow, and they don't have the muscle mass to strike with much force in return. Fast escape as a method of survival has enabled birds to become the most successful vertebrate on earth.

Flight is an automatic response in birds to fear. No thought process goes into action and no alternative action is considered. Their "mind set" has been programmed through heredity to take flight immediately whenever there is even a possiblity of a threatening situation occurring. Birds have no choice; no other response is available; flight is the only answer.

In the wild immediate flight from every danger is effective, but what happens to the bird in captivity where no escape is possible? What happens when fear dominates their mind?

Fear prevents birds from thinking and acting normally. Fear can dominate every emotion, every behavior characteristic, and sometimes even interferes with basic instincts such as eating, preening, reproduction and feeding their young. Everything suffers until fear abates. Unsolved fear offers pet birds a poor to disastrous life.

People put more fear into birds than guns do.

Fear is the main barrier to birds becoming excellent pets.

Removing fear can successfully be accomplished by any average person. Read pages 35 to 60.

3   BIRD BEHAVIOR
A Learning Experience

Early on, when first practicing bird medicine, I had a very enlightening conversation with a 22 year old man who had been blind since birth. He was seeking veterinary care for Jasper, his sick cockatiel.

Almost before he could tell me the bird's problem, I started quizzing him about his feelings towards birds as a pet. It surprised me that a person without vision could enjoy a bird. Birds' value, so much, I thought depended upon being seen. Now, this man was explaining to me that the bonding between the bird and him resulted from their needing each other, and a deep-seated relationship continually reinforced through physical contact. The high point of Jasper's day was sitting on his owner's arm to be petted. (I believe that his owner enjoyed it just as much.)

Always near, the bird woke him in the morning, was an almost constant companion during the day, and in the evenings complained when the lights weren't turned off at the regular time.

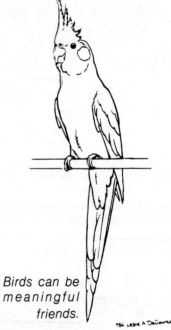

Birds can be meaningful friends.

He told me that returning Jasper to perfect health was uppermost in his mind.

How could he tell Jasper was sick? I knew he couldn't observe the droppings, the water or food consumption, a change in activity, or if the bird sat with feathers ruffled. The answer was simply that he knew his bird well, and that something was wrong.

The personable young man laughed as he explained his bird's likes and dislikes; how cold showers excited him; how a change in weather could be anticipated from his behavior; that noisy jet aircrafts landing and taking off at O'Hare Airfield made him nervous, and how some foods gave him a gassy stomach.

"You might think you were watching a comedy act," he said, "if you looked into my room and saw a blind person talking freely to a bird, who was intently listening as if understanding each word."

He thought I should know, and that I should emphasize to every bird owner the value of communicating with their bird. Birds respond so positively to our talking, singing, or whistling that it could be their most important recreation.

Obviously, this man and bird had become close friends. I learned then that he had the bird for five years, and that whenever the man felt depressed, the bird would react by sitting quietly on his shoulder. If he had something new, a package - clothing - new treat box - the bird was right there investigating. There were times to be quiet and times to play. If he wanted to be petted or scratched, Jasper would sit on his owner's hand and peck at his fingers; and when content, snuggle on his shoulder and quietly chatter. Nothing more needed to be said, the relationship was a most important part of his life.

Later, I learned from a friend of the blind man that the bird had appreciably helped his owner in relationships with people. He had become much less bitter about his sightlessness and now tried to be pleasant with everyone.

> Many other handicapped people can equally benefit from birds as companions.

Mimicking

Hearing birds of the parrot family talk in a voice resembling that of a person's seems almost unreal. This uncanny ability actually is part of their normal life style. Nature tells them to "follow the

25

leader." What their leader does they try hard to do. If a group of birds is sitting on a telephone wire and one flies away, they generally all fly away. If you've watched ducks in a pond, they stay in a group swimming first in one direction and then another, always staying with the lead duck.

Birds in the wild copy the leader and do things together because experience has taught them that there are survival advantages to living together as one.

Birds seem to enjoy a "copy cat" relationship. In a group of birds if one eats a new food, likely the others will follow. In a aviary, a parakeet learned how to swallow air so that his crop greatly distended. He seemed very proud and "showed off" this ability. Soon, other birds in the aviary learned the same trick and were ballooning their crop.

That birds can imitate our speech leaves one impressed and amazed.

Further, watching birds chew gum, untie knots, open cage doors, peel a grape, cough when people cough, say "hello" when we enter a room and "good-bye" when we leave seems beyond their capability, and yet they do all this and much more.

Like ducks in a pond, birds follow the leader.

Birds will only start mimicking our behavior when they feel they are part of our flock. They must look on the person doing the teaching as the leader—and then the game is "follow the leader."

Work and Play

Like the seven dwarfs in "Snow White and the Seven Dwarfs," birds happily start their work at dawn and continue until the sun sets every evening—and without pay! Constant activity exemplifies their way of life. Ever on the move, searching for food, defending their territory, constantly vigilant for enemies, preening, playing, vocalizing, looking for a mate—then courtship, nesting, feeding the young and migrating. No one would ever accuse birds of being lazy animals.

Never lazy, birds like to work.

Pet birds have the same energies for work and play as wild birds. Although not as lively in captivity, pet birds still thrive on being busy.

Flying and Not Flying

The marjority of the flight hours logged by birds involves their search for food—an exercise using both mental and physical activities. This may seem an impossible situation to duplicate, and indeed, even the largest aviary cannot allow for the amount of flying performed in the wild. Every cage limits flight. However, flight, while an asset, does not seem to be essential for the maintenance of normal health. Flying is a method of transportation which can be restricted without detrimental effects.

Work

Life in captivity could easily be monotonous. Because of this, bird owners will want to help provide work and play activities on a regular basis.

Food Gathering—

Except for actual flying, pet birds can go through all the stages of food gathering. By offering food for limited periods in the morning and evening, birds will develop the normal appetite. As feeding time approaches, excitement, vocalization, activity, and anticipation increase. These reactions continue until feeding time, and fulfill pet birds' needs for the food gathering process. Pertinent information is on pages 113 to 118.

Chewing—

soft wood perches, branches, hang toys, pine cones, clothes—pins, pencils, spoons, cardboard and bones. Pertinent information on pages 81, 135 to 137.

Eating—

foods which require beak activities—cakes, bars, nuggets, seeds, nuts and biscuits.

Feather care—

preening, lubricating, arranging, cleaning, smoothing and bathing.

Body Exercise—

with chains, ropes, ladders, swings, and rings which encourage acrobatics.

Whenever birds work they respond positively. Birds who have work are much more active, communicative, responsive, observant and alert.

Play

Birds frequently indulge in activities that seem to have no practical purpose, but appear to be simply done for its own sake—play.

In captivity, birds can concentrate on the things they enjoy—singing, talking, acrobatics, tricks, investigating and interaction with people.

Sure sounds like play to me!

Playing is part of a bird's day.

Suspicion

Birds have specialized in being suspicious animals. They have perfected it to an art. Their superior vision and their intelligence give them a keen sense of what's going on around them. In the wild, these attributes help them survive. Life depends upon recognizing dangers early and escaping. Their "radar" is turned on all the time.

Besides a visual recognition of objects or animals that might be harmful to them, birds' suspicion broadens to include an alertness to even the "feeling" of danger. If a person or animal is present who has a hostile attitude toward birds, they are likely to perceive this as a danger and react accordingly.

Always watchful.

Mirrors and Shiny Objects

The fascination that birds have for mirrors relates to their strong desire to have friends and relationships. When they see their reflection, it is like seeing another bird. Much to their delight the reflecting bird seems friendly and attentive.

If given a choice, birds would choose people as friends rather than mirrors. Mirrors, though, can be tough competition. The reflected bird is always present whenever the bird looks for him. A sort of constant companion that's there on demand. Easily the reflection can become the best friend and the owner only a secondary friend.

With no mirror or other reflecting surface present, pet birds focus attention on their owner.

Escape

Do birds constantly seek escape? No!

Through three million years of evolution, birds have solved all their problems by flying away from them. At any sound, movement, or strangeness, the bird's alarm system would immediately react and send the bird into flight. This system was so successful that birds never had to become cunning or look for other answers. Flight remains as their compelling solution. As a result, they have limited ability to adjust to those things that frighten them, but adjust well to life in captivity when in a consistently pleasant environment.

Newly purchased birds are frequently fearful animals and should be expected to attempt to escape. Until fear has been alleviated, escape is always foremost in their mind. More information on pages 22 and 23.

Every year hundreds of tame birds "fly away" into the trees adjacent to their homes. Their solo flight into the wild soon becomes a fearful experience. The strangeness sends them to the security and safety of tall trees. Fear and confusion keeps them from returning to their owners.

Some manage to return to their owner when hunger develops. However, hunger cannot be depended upon. When fear becomes intense, it overrides the sensation of hunger. These birds, then, have to be trapped or caught. Spraying them with water from the underside wets their feathers, impeding their ability to fly and in this way makes capture easier.

Pet birds taken out-of-doors should always have their flight feathers cut. Even tame birds fly away.

Fighters or Bluffers

Basically, birds' hostile activities can be summed up as bluff. Pet birds are not warriors. They have "big mouths," and display meanness, but don't carry through. It's mostly show—and they do a good job of it.

Lovers not fighters.

Behind this type of behavior comes some very good logic. Fighters need relatively large, heavy bodies, strong bones and an ability to withstand repeated blows. Birds have none of these qualifications. Their light weight body and thin bones are designed for fliers not fighters.

Also, if you're not a fighter, you had better control your anger. Like poker players, birds bluff, gambling with controlled minds, constantly judging and adjusting to their opponents. They're "cool." They express themselves in ritualized postures, movements, and calls that serve to repel or intimidate without actual combat. Thus, birds rarely allow themselves to become aggressive.

On occasion, one may come across a bird with a dominant, aggressive type personality. In captivity, this bird may show its aggression by attacking with little, if any, provocation. Fortunately, this type bird is less frequently encountered than the more passive type.

Important in their social life is an arrangement commonly called a "peck order." A ranking takes place between all the individuals in a group. Each bird assumes a place in the social hierarchy starting with the most dominant, the highest position, and following in order to the lowest or most submissive. To show superiority or to rise to a higher level, they will take aggressive action in the form of threatening gestures or biting at the one they are challenging.

Following the natural order, some birds may challenge their owner in the same fashion to raise their rank on the social ladder.

"Listen you big ox!
I came first."

Scolding

Like a school teacher trying to improve the behavior of a student, birds scold. They become very indignant when certain things happen or don't happen as the case may be. The tone of their voice changes and becomes louder than normal.

Scolding shows a side of their personality that an owner might not understand. Birds expect a certain consistency in their lives. Once routines are established they anticipate events to happen and if they don't it becomes upsetting to them and they tell you about it. Seemingly unimportant happenings to the owner may be significant to the bird. Maybe they are used to the lights being turned out in their room at a certain time; or the cage routinely covered at bedtime; or breakfast fed at a specific time. For a bird, these events might be worth squalking about.

Vacations

The convenience of leaving birds at home on weekends or for vacations works favorably for owners and their birds. Being left alone is well accepted—as long as fresh food, water, and daily observation by an interested party are available.

When no one can come to your home to care for your bird, then board your bird at a local pet store or veterinary hospital. Having experienced people care for your bird is the wisest choice.

If you want your bird to travel with you, then you'll need to acclimate your bird to change. Take him with you on a car ride, to visit a neighbor, or even to work about once a week. Have other people hand feed, talk to, and touch him. Each experience should be pleasant and bring some type of reward. Your bird will begin to enjoy the excitement of travel.

"World traveler" but vacations may be troublesome.

Some precautions should be taken —keep flight feathers trimmed so that flight is impossible. Don't have your bird loose in your car with the window open. Birds become overheated when left in direct sunlight or on a hot day when denied ventilation—as in a closed car.

4 TAMING

Remember
to

Help Me!

...and I'll be
a great pet!

Are you gifted with common sense? If so, taming your bird should be fun.

Consider these:

 The average home provides an ideal environment for pet birds.

 Birds are naturally friendly animals.

 We win a bird's friendship by showing ourselves as consistent, caring people.

 As soon as birds lose their fear of us they—

—enjoy receiving our attention

—like to be touched

—want to eat out of our hand

—willingly communicate (vocalize) with us

—become curious about almost everything

—Fear of people is the main barrier to birds becoming loving pets. Newly purchased birds are almost always full of fear.

The First Days In A New Home

Most birds being tamed have just been purchased. Owners will first want to help their bird adapt successfully to his new environment.

Preparatory Measures Before Taming Starts

A welcome home celebration for your new bird won't be needed. In fact, noise and confusion may initially create a fearful environment for your new pet.

Some things in homes might at first be threatening. So the first few days will be of special importance, and precautions will have to be taken to allow for an adjustment to a new environment.

Young birds and birds that have been handled adjust more quickly than older ones. **As a general rule, allow 2-3 days for young birds and a week for older ones before taming begins.**

Protection

So that a new bird is not overwhelmed by a new environment, the top and sides of the cage are covered—leaving only a front view exposed.

Memory

Animals that have to survive in the wild have excellent memories for bad things that happen to them. Not only do elephants never forget, neither do birds. If birds are ever teased, hit or frightened, either purposely or accidentally, they won't soon forget the incident.

Diet

Continue the same diet that your bird was fed before you obtained him. NO CHANGE FOR ABOUT ONE WEEK! Changes in foods which seem of no consequence might keep birds from approaching their food. Be certain that when you begin adding new foods that it is done gradually, and that your bird continues to eat well.

Water

The most essential food in your bird's life is water. For this reason, a person can easily understand the need to always keep clean fresh water in his drinking cup.

Food Consumption and Droppings

Until birds are well adjusted to their new home, food consumption should be closely watched. Fear and stress can "kill" a bird's normal appetite. With no appetite they may eat insufficient food or none at all. Because birds have relatively short intestinal tracts and because food passes through rapidly, the volume of droppings is an excellent index of food consumption.

A normal parakeet will have approximately thirty to forty droppings per day. If that many droppings are counted every 24 hours, you can be certain your bird is eating well. Less than thirty droppings could be cause for concern.

Change the cage paper daily for health reasons and to note the number and character of droppings.

Paper to Cover the Bottom of the Cage

Paper, whether newspaper, brown paper, paper towels, or other types, not only serves as a readily available disposable cover for the bottom of the cage, but also has the advantage of allowing the droppings to be easily viewed. Likewise, by stacking several sheets of paper, the daily routine of cage cleaning will simply involve removing the top sheet and disposing of it. The droppings can be quickly checked at this time.

Behavior Near Pet Birds

Birds can give us a lesson in observing and understanding body language. They study a person's every gesture, expression, movement and action as if their lives depended upon them. They notice everything and read a person's attitude very well.

Avoid approaching strange birds carelessly. A rapid advance, running, and quick movements easily frighten them. **A person's actions and gestures should not be intimidating, threatening or provoking.**

Personal Appearance

When I think of birds, their superb vision always enters my mind. Yet even with keen eyesight, under certain conditions, they can fail to recognize their owners. When appearance has been altered, especially if it affects the face or head, they can be confused as to your identity.

When birds see their owner wearing a hat and coat, they may believe it is a stranger. Even the growth of a beard can change a man's identity sufficiently to confuse birds. Costume parties are not for birds!

A Daily Routine

Certain procedures for maintenance need to be performed daily—cage cover removed in the morning, fresh water given, cage paper changed, breakfast, dinner and treats fed, taming schedule repeated, and cage cover applied in the evening.

When bird owners perform these functions in the same order each day birds accept them best. This type of regularity allows birds to know what is going to happen next. So if possible, make it a habit of taking care of birds in the same order and approximately same time daily.

Also, the routine a person establishes for himself becomes very familiar to birds. Birds will understand what time you arise each morning and that you sleep late on Sunday morning.

Sleep

Darkening the cage with a cover for 8 - 12 hours at night provides an easy way of compelling birds to get sufficient sleep. Plenty of rest helps the adjustment process and serves to protect a bird's physical and mental health. The cover needs to be dense or thick enough to provide darkness.

Noise

While your bird is becoming familiar with the sounds of your home, try to keep offending noises at a minimum — door slamming, loud radios, and dogs' barking. After a week all ordinary sounds should be well accepted.

Probably the most upsetting noise to birds would be those sounds produced by people arguing, screaming, shouting, or fighting. Just as in the wild, any sound of alarm makes all animals uneasy and fearful.

Cage Height

A cage should give your bird the feeling of height. The height of a cage in a room has a remarkable effect on birds. A cage on the floor causes birds to be nervous and fearful. **Move the cage to a table or counter height and most birds will be satisfied.**

Cage Location

Birds need to be kept in an area of the house where they can view and become acquainted with normal household activities and sounds, and begin to feel comfortable in the presence of people.

While birds tolerate many hours of isolation well, they need daily socialization with people.

The family room or any other room with plenty of activity would probably be ideal.

Toys and Mirrors

Seeing their reflection in a mirror or shiny object distracts birds and seriously interferes with taming. Some toys have the same affect. It's best to keep toys and mirrors out of the cage during the taming process.

Escape and Flying Loose

If a bird becomes loose in a room, be cautious. Rushing to grab him may create fear in his life that will take months to overcome.

First, **the owner should never do anything to frighten birds.** So, if you are going to catch your bird, you're best off wearing a disguise. It doesn't take much to fool a bird, so an old fishing hat, pulled low on

the head, plus an unfamiliar smock is adequate. Do not speak during the retrieving process because your bird may recognize your voice. Place the bird back in his cage; leave the room; take off your disguise and return. He will never know that **you** caught him.

Second, **don't catch birds with your bare hand.** Your hands are supposed to be a friendly source of affection and food. Cover your hands with a towel or gloves.

Capturing a loose bird with a net can be very effective. The owner will still not want to associate himself with the process, and would use the precautions mentioned in Escape and Flying Loose.

Body Weight

Feathers effectively hide a bird's weight just as a baggy suit might hide a person's weight. For this reason, weight changes cannot be detected on birds by visual observation. **Frequent weight checks are advisable, especially on a new pet.**

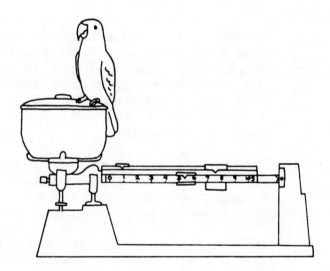

Communicating—An Important Part of Friendship

Just as birds constantly have you under visual surveillance, they also listen to every sound you make. Therefore, you continually have an acoustic (hearing) relationship with your bird—so important in taming.

Birds' Need: Birds don't vocalize just to hear themselves; they talk and sing their way through life because it is an important function in the wild. Communications are involved in reproduction, defense, identification, food gathering, training their young, social functions and their own enjoyment. When vocalizations consume such a large share of birds' time and energy, and is part of nearly all their daily activities, it can be presumed to be a vital function. Birds, then, need to vocalize and receive feed back.

Qualifications: Pet birds may have egos as big as humans! They crave attention! The main method to attract attention is through vocalizing—singing, talking and other utterances. They want to be the center of activity! They like to be heard and want a response. (Maybe they feel like rock stars and think they should be on center stage).

Procedure: Helping pet birds to become good friends partially depends upon an owner talking, humming, whispering, singing, whistling or in any way communicating with his birds.

This gives birds a happier, more complete, more natural life. As in relationships between human beings, communication between owner and birds helps build understanding.

Vocalizing to birds may seem one-sided, but the tone of your voice, the enthusiasm, the excitement and the rate are all being heard and interpreted. Even a lack of conversation sends a message.

Birds learn to know the significance of the sounds people vocalize - "good morning", "food", "treats", "pretty bird", etc. They certainly can't understand our language, but maybe, have a feeling for what we say and know who said it.

Birds hear every sound you make and every word you speak.

In fact, any sort of communication, directly or indirectly, has a stimulating effect on them.

Like a person who claims he sings best in the shower, most birds are definitely influenced in their vocalization by environmental conditions. Most noticeable, though, is a bird's response to sounds. Canaries sing more when in an area of activity, and parrots talk more in your presence or when you have company.

(When I tap on my desk with a pencil, my cockatiel perks up, starts to walk around excitedly, and he responds by tapping his beak against his perch.)

More information on pages 15, 16 and 17.

Feeding A Hungry Bird

Birds' Need: Food availability governs the lives of birds.

Bird Behavior: Birds instinctively know that survival depends upon food gathering. When hunger develops, the need to eat takes precedence over everything else. Even in the face of danger they will gamble for what they know they need. They subjugate their instinctive suspicions and fear to reach food. Through a learning process birds begin to be convinced that they need us, and that their owners are kind, benevolent people.

Owner's Role: Feeding a hungry animal is always a sure method to begin a friendship.

Everyone seems to feel that the answer to making a fearful bird love you, is through food. But providing food is not enough. The solution lies in regulating feedings and having a consistent caring attitude. The following example will make this clear.

Friends

Being good to a stray puppy or taming a pet bird, is it the same?

A very understandable answer might begin with thinking about a frightened, stray dog that you have noticed in the prairie in back of your home. From a distance the dog appears to be young, terribly underweight and so nervous and terrified, that he seems to be startled, and on his toes, ready to run for any reason.

*Feeding a hungry animal is a sure way
to begin a friendship.*

You decide to place some food in an area where he is likely to find it, and then return to your house to observe from the window.

During the next week you repeat this procedure daily, and find that the puppy now anticipates the feedings and will distance himself only a few feet from you. A few more days of patience, sitting quietly and letting the dog become familiar with you, and he will probably eat out of your hand. He needs to begin to trust you.

With more feedings, playing together, and pleasant conversation, a friendship develops.

The puppy's love of his new found friend can now be extended to others.

Procedure: The same basic technique as decribed on the "wild" dog works well on birds.

Start by feeding two or three meals daily, and removing the food dishes from the eating area between meals. Leave food available for a minimum of ten minutes, and a maximum of one hour. The length of time is not critical, but there should be some consistency from day to day. Your bird might miss his first meal, but after that, he will fill his crop in a short time. Birds are not dumb!

Contrary to established thinking, birds do not "starve to death" when fed two meals daily. In fact, the degree of hunger brought about by separate feedings is only sufficient to develop a hearty appetite.

As feedings are continued day after day, birds feel the regularity and begin to look forward to you bringing food. Birds soon learn that they need you. More information on page 116.

Rewards and Treats

Like other animals, birds respond to rewards. About the only type of prize a bird will take is food, and then, only if hungry or it happens to be a particular food that he loves. If hunger and favorite foods are combined into a response program, the results can be very positive.

Occasions for the use of rewards could be:

for talking

for shaking hands

for leaving the cage

for returning to the cage

for doing tricks

Friends

There is at least one time when giving a reward would not be beneficial. If a bird is noisy, you would not give him a treat to make him quiet. A reward at this time would only make the bird believe the reward came because of his noise. The result would be a noisier bird.

Touch Taming for Parakeets and Other Small Birds

The EZ-TAME CAGE—a long needed development for the taming of parakeets.

Taming proceeds the fastest when <u>physical contact takes place between trainer and bird.</u> This type of taming benefits birds because they rapidly lose their fear of people and quickly become a friend of the owner. Owners enjoy the transition of watching a fearful bird become a loving pet.

Birds Need: Birds can become loving pets, but they need assistance.

Bird Behavior: If pet birds are left alone they will remain wild. Even though they are friendly animals they will not depart from their regular conduct unless obliged by circumstances. Adjustment to new situations can occur rapidly as long as no harm comes to them.

Birds natural behavior blends with touch taming as long as there is no hostility or teasing.

Procedure: Touch taming for parakeets and other small birds can now be performed in an EZ-TAME CAGE with TAME-IN NOOK ™. Since this is the only cage of its type on the market, the following explanation decribes the use of the EZ-TAME CAGE.*

Parakeets are placed in a relatively small but ample cage for the short taming period.

The top and sides of the cage are solid to prevent stress and distraction. Its light weight and small size allow the owner to tame the bird almost anywhere. Taming can even be done while the owner watches television. This approach makes taming easy and enjoyable.

The design of the cage allows the bird being tamed to be corralled into a small nook—just large enough to turn around.

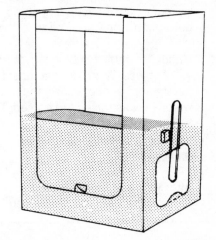

*TAME-IN NOOK is
the shaded area.*

Since the nook is actually part of the taming cage, birds are not traumatized by unnecessary handling.

*The EZ-TAME CAGE ™ is available from your pet store, veterinarian or Lafeber Co.

Bird owners are instructed to slide their hand into the nook, and will find that after the initial surprise and fear pass that their hand will be treated no differently than if it were a harmless object.

With the owner's hand in the limited space of the nook, it's easy to have the bird step onto his finger. This is the start of a desirable contact between the bird and his owner.

Familiarity and confidence build on the length and frequency of contact.

The taming nook should be used 4-5 times daily for three to five minutes each time—more often and longer periods would be fine.

The instructions accompanying the EZ-TAME CAGE have the following explanation:

In order to by-pass birds' fear of people, the EZ-TAME Method of Taming acquaints your bird with your hand as if it were a small, independent object—not a part of you. (Birds get to know only your hand in the TAME-IN NOOK.)

Under favorable conditions, your bird will accept your hand as harmless. To produce a most ideal environment for your parakeet to accept your hand, the conditions of the nest in which he was raised are copied. The TAME-IN NOOK effectively duplicates these circumstances by offering a dimly lit chamber. Under this arrangement your bird will be most receptive.

After your bird has accepted your hand as friendly, it's easy to carry that feeling over to you.

Instead of just accepting the owner's hand, the goal is to have parakeets look forward to a visit by the hand. This is accomplished by allowing parakeets to develop a good appetite, and then to hand feed him in the nook.

When the owner's hand is completely accepted, the nook will no longer be needed. The owner can now reach into the cage and hand feed many times a day.

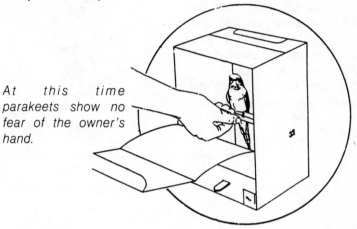

At this time parakeets show no fear of the owner's hand.

A most interesting event takes place. Parakeets now see that the hand is connected to a person. Wonder of wonders—when parakeets have learned not to be afraid of the owner's hand they accept the whole person as friendly.

With the bird sitting on your hand you raise him out of the cage and complete the taming with him in and out of the cage.

This series of events take place in 1 to 4 weeks. Progress will be seen daily.

Because the birds being tamed never have to be removed from their cage during taming, almost anyone from seven to seventy can use the procedure.

Before proceeding with the EZ-TAME Method of taming, **it is important to have your pet store or veterinarian clip your bird's flight feathers.** If your bird escapes, this precaution could prevent a serious injury. At the same time the tips of the toenails could be smoothed off, and, if needed, the beak blunted.

Contact Taming For Large Birds

Large birds present some danger to owners because of the possibility of biting. Contact taming is recommended only for those people who have had experience handling larger birds.

Plan: The same plan is applied in this procedure as with the EZ-TAME CAGE—only the setting is different.

Preparation: Have your bird's flight feathers cut, beak blunted, and toe nails clipped.

Pick an area just slightly larger than needed for the owner to sit on the floor and be comfortable. In actual size about 3' to 4' square. The area in a home most suitable could be a closet, end of hallway, shower stall, or something like a playpen or box with straight smooth sides that will accommodate both you and your bird.

A small area keeps the bird confined and close to you. Larger areas invite cat and mouse games. Repeated "round-up-time" causes short tempers and hostile attitudes.

Close proximity to the owner causes birds to accept the situation and adjust to it. The main precaution is for the owner not to do anything that would be interpreted by the bird as hostile.

Procedure: Plan for each taming session to last 15-30 minutes and repeat daily or more often to make good progress.

Getting Birds Out Of Their Cage

To work with a bird he must be out of the cage, and this at time presents problems. If you reach into the cage to catch him, you probably will be making the bird even more fearful of you, and if done repeatedly, much harm can be done. For this situation use a cage which has a bottom that can easily be removed. With the bottom out, the cage is laid on it's side in the confinement area. In a short time the bird will wander out.

The owner now carefully gets into the pen with the bird, and assumes a comfortable position.

Step 1—   Waiting For Fear To Alleviate

                 At first the bird will be fearful and all his mental and physical efforts will go toward finding a way to escape. It's only after these thoughts begin to wane that any progress can be made. Initially, then, it is a matter of time— maybe 15-30 minutes—before any progress is possible.

                 The bird has to feel that he is not being attacked, or being put in a defensive situation. We want the bird to feel that everything is okay, that the person confined with him is not a predator, aggressor, or, in any way harmful.

Step 2—   Contact

                 The bird is tested from time to time by sliding your hand near, waiting, and repeating the procedure until the bird steps onto your hand. Wait again, let him feel comfortable.

Step 2—   For the first sitting this may be as far as you go, but it is real progress. At future taming sessions your bird will accept your hand more readily, although each time, initially, he will think of escape.

Step 3—   Raise Birds Off The Floor

                 When you start to elevate your hand, he may step off. By repeated experiences he will remain on your hand.

Step 4—   Using Height As An Advantage

At first you may be sitting on the floor with the bird, but later on you may find that by being higher—either kneeling or standing—birds will step on your hand quicker. The explanation involves the insecurity a bird feels with another living thing over him. Birds will compromise their fear of your hand to get to a higher position.

If he starts to walk up your forearm, elevate your hand and forearm. That way you can keep him from walking to your shoulder.

Since the first goal is to make birds relate to your hand, allowing birds to climb to your shoulder lets them avoid your hand. Also, until your bird is fully tame—your ear or neck might be bitten.

Step 5—   "Stair Stepping"

Climbing comes natural to members of the parrot family. So, parrots quickly take to stepping up from a finger on a hand to the finger on the other hand in a sort of climb the ladder exercise. With your bird on your index finger facing you—press your finger from the opposite hand against his chest. This pressure generally causes birds to step up onto whatever is creating the pressure. Soon the action feels comfortable to him and he will continue "stair-stepping" from one finger to the other as you rotate hands.

Step 6—   Freedom and Owner Involvement

The following days repeat the procedure, only add more personal contact. As the bird allows—touch the bird on the chest and back, and try working toward the head.

If during any of this time the bird wants to move away, let him. Don't try to physically confine him as the result will be fear and distrust. The more freedom he gets, the more trust and confidence he will have in his owner.

The object will be to have the bird freely step on your hand or forearm, to let you scratch his head and back, and have confidence that he is in no danger.

5 CAGE, EXERCISE AREA, AND FURNISHINGS

What's Best For Pet Birds?

After 2,000 years, we are still discovering better ways to provide for birds. Current information that many of our birds suffer psychological problems caused by improper housing has precipitated the need for new and innovative designs in bird cages.

How does a bird owner know if he purchased the best cage for his bird? Is the cage large enough? Does the cage provide all the essentials for a happy life in captivity? What is the purpose of a cage? How can a cage damage a bird mentality?

Not until the current era of birds becoming personal pets did anyone begin to be concerned with the full effect of caging. That's not surprising because birds have never complained about their housing. And that may mean the problem is partially their fault. They seem to accept whatever conditions are imposed on them. They always look content. So how are bird owners to know that cages are causing adverse effects?

Owners accept total guardianship for their pet.

61

Living Area For Pet Birds

Introducing the subject of cages for birds may be similar to talking about housing for people. We require homes to live in, but would rather not be confined to them permanently, no matter how nice. Birds have to be caged, but also desire freedom.

> Cages should be considered a home for pet birds when their activity needs to be restricted. But never for permanent confinement.

The Danger of Cages

Let me explain. Most people probably don't realize that continuous confinement in cages can create serious psychological problems for birds. Birds may appear to be content and living a normal life, but appearances can be deceiving. Birds often develop a phychosis from caging and become "goofy." It may ordinarily go unnoticed unless they begin acting abnormally—such as plucking their feathers out, or screaming. I'm not saying that pet birds have to fly loose, or that cages aren't important. I'm concerned when birds are placed in cages and then never leave.

Pet birds need a roomy cage, daily freedom, and a play area outside of the cage. How much cage space does a parakeet need?

The minimum cage size for parakeet housing should allow ample room for stretching, hopping, jumping, climbing, acrobatics and to hold interesting toys. To be more specific, their 12 inch wing span

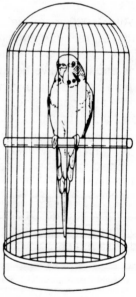

Birds can develop a cage psychosis.

should be accommodated by a cage at least 14 inches wide. To keep their long tail from touching the floor of the cage requires perches to be six inches off the floor and approximately the same distance from either end of the cage. Ordinarily, there would be two perches about six inches apart. Total length of cage would measure 18 inches or more. A reasonable minimum height would be approximately 12 inches.

Larger birds need cages proportionately roomier.

If birds have two or more hours of freedom outside, do they need a big cage?

Because birds want to be active whether in or out of a cage, the size of the cage is always significant. Every cage should be of sufficient size to give birds room to hop or move from perch to perch, for acrobatics, stretch their wings and to hold toys.

The requirement for large size cages can be compromised if birds have time outside of their cage. A period of two hours a day would be minimum.

What kind of freedom does a bird need?

The opportunity to leave the cage and climb to the top probably will give most birds adequate freedom. Cages with flat tops can be equipped with play areas—ladders, swings, ropes, toys, perches and places for food and water dishes. Since birds always want to go to height, the top of a cage is really an ideal free area for pet birds.

Birds need the freedom of being outside of their cage.

What about exercise areas?

Play pens and exercise areas are carried by pet stores.

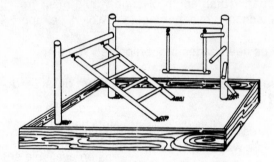

How can a cage help promote companionship—socialization—friendship?

A few cages now on the market have been designed to conveniently give birds freedom. The top may open or the sides swing out or down.

Fear from a loud noise may cause a dog to scurry under the bed or hide where he feels safe, but what do pet birds do when they are frightened? They also would like to hide, but in a cage where are they to go?

Safety and security are always of utmost importance to birds. (If you lived inside their delicate bodies you'd want to avoid threatening situations, too.) Experience has shown, though, that elaborate measures are not necessary. Anything that would act as a visual barrier between them and the source of concern provides sufficient protection. Birds feel safe when they <u>think</u> they are well hidden—when they have a <u>feeling</u> that their enemies cannot find them.

Dr. William Dilger tells of an incident which occured in the Ornithology Laboratory at Cornell University. A graduate student had a research project in which he had to closely observe the behavior of a group of wild birds. The birds had successfully been collected and were housed and allowed to free fly in an 8' × 10' area. To collect the desired data the student placed a chair just inside the door where he would sit quietly and observe their actions.

The project initially failed. When the student sat in the room the birds were constantly uneasy. At times they would hysterically attempt to escape, flying recklessly around and blindly crashing into the walls. Their feathers were being broken and damaged, and their wings, head and body bruised. The more the student observed, the worse the birds became. The more he stayed away, the calmer they were.

When the student finally discussed the problem with Dr. Dilger, a plan was formulated. Across from the door and a couple of feet from the wall a rope was stretched near the ceiling. Burlap sacks were hung from the rope, and a perch was placed behind the sacks.

Within three days the student could procede with his study, with the birds almost ignoring him. Now, with safety behind the sacks the birds felt secure to come within a few feet of the student.

In retrospect, all the birds needed was an available security area.

For practical purposes a piece of material hung down from the top of the cage so that if desired a bird may hide behind it, works well.

Only One Pet Per Cage.

If the purpose of keeping a bird in your home is to have a pet, then maintaining each bird separately is essential.

When two birds have the companionship of each other, they don't need you. (Just as a mirror in a cage can hurt relationships.) Further, two birds together can impede taming and training, and, if anything, they tend to become wild.

Placing two birds in one cage always risks incompatability. The appearance of harmony, especially in lovebirds, may be deceiving. One may dominate

Birds need to love their owner not another bird.

the other, guard the food dish and physically injure the lesser, and yet they sit with their heads together as if in love. The subordinate bird eventually shows signs of harrassment, weight loss, weakness and plucked feathers. Separation is the only solution.

Should food cups be in or out of the pet bird's cage?

Having meals out of the cage can help change a bird's attitude on eating and toward his owner.

Having birds leave their cage is the first step to opening up a whole new world.

Birds that would eat only certain foods enlarge their appetites to include many types of food. Eating out of the cage allows them to be more expansive and also to regain their natural curiosity.

Feeding outside of the cage has the advantage to the owner of making mealtime much more convenient. The dishes are easy to fill, empty, and clean.

Cage Paper

Emphasis needs to be placed on the importance of the cage paper and the need to change it daily. Bird droppings have no odor, and without an offensive smell, it is not likely that the pet owner will feel the need to change the cage paper frequently. The proper motivation must come through an understanding and realization of the basic facts.

The first function of the cage paper is to collect the feces and allow you to dispose of them easily and conveniently. Manure building up in the bird's cage—even though it has no appreciable odor—allows bacteria to multiply and results in an unnecessary danger to the bird. As the waste material dries and becomes powdery, currents of air pick up this dust and spread it into the environment contaminating the bird's food and air. Bird droppings are fairly dry within 48 hours. The recommendation, then, is to change the cage paper at 24 hour intervals.

The second reason for changing the cage paper daily is equal in importance to the first. The bird's droppings function as an effective indicator in measuring the bird's health. When the paper is changed frequently, fresh droppings are constantly observed. If the feces are allowed to mound up, interpretation and evaluation is impossible.

CHANGE CAGE PAPER DAILY

The psittasine groups of birds, particularly, enjoy clipping and wadding the paper, possibly as part of a nesting habit. Eating the cage paper reflects a depraved appetite and a veterinarian should be consulted.

Often grit is fed to a pet bird by covering the floor of the cage with "gravel paper"—paper cut to fit the bottom of the cage which has grit adhered to it—or laying grit loosely on the bottom of the cage. Neither method is an acceptable way of providing grit for the bird. First of all, grit is on the floor where it will be mixed and eaten with the droppings. Secondly, the grit supplied loose or with these papers is not the required grit-mineral mixture.

The other disadvantage to gravel paper is that it must be purchased and a considerable quantity used over the period of one year. The economics are likely to discourage someone from changing the cage paper daily. Newspaper or some other disposable paper will function just as well.

Cage Cover

In the colonial house, birds were in a position of prominence and needed to be protected against the changes in temperatures which occurred as the fires died out during the night. The cage was covered by a heavy cloth or blanket to help retain the heat until morning.

The change in our lifestyle has had both advantages and disadvantages for the bird, and the cage cover is involved. The bird needs the cover today as badly as he did in colonial times, but for entirely different reasons. In our modern living, we have created another problem for birds.

Our sophisticated housing has effectively destroyed some of the environmental influences that helped control the bird's cyclic metabolism.

In the modern home, the temperature, humidity and photoperiods (number of hours of light in the day) are maintained almost stable summer and winter. In effect, there no longer is a change in seasons for the bird to help stimulate and regulate the endocrine (hormone), reproductive and integumentary (skin and feathers, beak and nails) systems.

Another problem created from today's lifestyle involves the number of hours of sleep allowed the bird each night. Because of their susceptibility to light, birds can only sleep when it is dark. Although they will close their eyes during the daylight hours as if sleeping, the presence of the light is still stressing to their system. A room which is light until midnight and re-illuminated at 6:00 A.M., creates only six hours of sleep for the bird. If this is continued night after night, the stress of insufficient sleep will allow physical and neurological problems to develop.

Therefore, cage covers or other methods of controlling the photoperiods are now needed. The bird's cage should be cloaked with a light tight cover sufficiently well to make it dark. The light should be regulated to correspond to approximately the number of hours of daylight in a day.

Perch

A bird's entire life is spent either standing or flying. The thought of standing most of one's life creates mental pictures of sore, aching feet and legs. A bird not only stands all day long, but also sleeps in the same position with his claws locked around the perch. The only time in his life span, 10–77 years, the bird is off its feet is when the hen is nesting. When not flying, the bird may walk, but generally jumps from place to place, which is a further insult to the already stressed locomotion system.

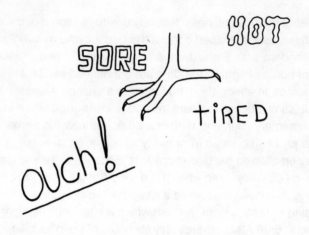

The material a bird stands on does make a difference. Should the surface be smooth or rough? Should the perch be hard or soft? Should the perch be flexible or rigid? The shape may also be questioned. The answer to these questions will prevent a few of the leg and foot problems that bother our birds.

Shapes

Although we think of something round when the word "perch" is spoken, there are many shapes. A variety of shapes in the bird's perches is probably more important than a number of round perches of various diameters. The goal must be to have even distribution of weight on the toes and feet in order to prevent pressure sores. Having the toes grip different size and shape perches conditions all parts of the foot.

Shapes:

Round
Oval
Square
Rectangular

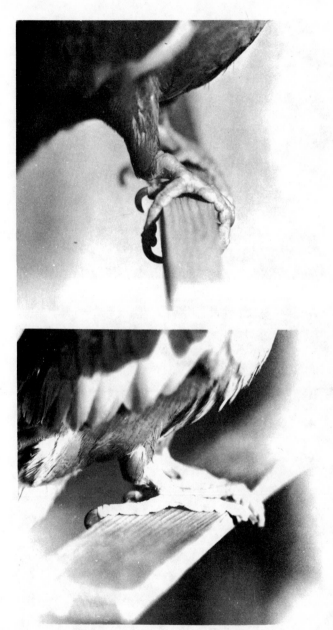

Notice the difference in the pressure points between the types of perches.

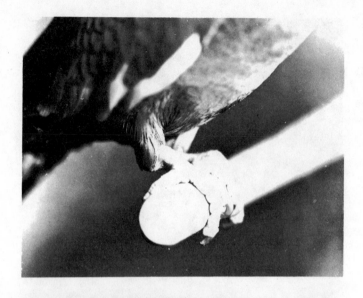

Flat (Birds sometimes prefer to sit with their toes extended on a flat, wide perch. Any board placed across the cage can easily provide for this need.)

Soft Perches

With the frequency that foot problems have been encountered in pet birds, it is advisable to have a soft perch in the cage which the bird may use if he desires:

Padded—cotton, cork or carpeting or other soft material

Wrapped—with paper towel, flannel or felt

Soft hose—as suggested under "non-rigid"

Softwoods—white pine for lovebirds, conures and parrots

—balsa wood for parakeets and cocktails

Rigid

In observations of aviary birds where both rigid and non-rigid perches were used, the birds about equally divided their time between the two. Both types should be provided for your bird's use.

Non-Rigid

As nature has provided swaying branches, non-rigid perches help to absorb the shock and impact of a bird's landing. As the bird made its adaptation for flight, the bony skeleton became delicate, and therefore a cushioned stop is helpful. A hose stretched across the cage makes an ideal perch, especially if composed of soft rubber or soft plastic.

Swings
String or rope stretched across cage
Perches with a spring end
Branch with small twigs on it

Branches

I've told many first clients that they should carry a pocket knife. After the surprise comes off their faces tell them that it's to be used daily to cut twigs off of bushes or trees for their bird.

Birds enjoy green twigs or small branches more for beak activities than a perch. The bark provides a challenge to birds, and they strip it off enthusiastically. Some birds chew at the underlying soft wood.

The entertainment seems to be over when the wood has become exposed, and they await a fresh new branch. Thus, collecting a small twig or branch becomes an almost daily ritual. I doubt that any commerical toy provides any better beak exercise or entertainment value than fresh branches and twigs.

Branches and twigs used as perches have certain advantages for birds. The irregularity of branches supplies a variety of shapes and sizes for birds to grip. This distributes their body weight to different parts of the toes and helps to prevent pressure sores.

Equipment—Bird Bath

Every bird deserves and needs to bathe. (See Feather Care). The type of apparatus that you will need will vary almost with the individual bird.

Saucer with Water

Any type of low saucer or pan is adequate. The problems faced with this type of bathing is that the bird, through his splashing and shaking, will throw droplets of water into the surrounding area and pretty well wet it down. Containers can be purchased to hang on the door of the cage, which are shielded so that the moisture is kept within the birdbath. For birds that are allowed out of their cages, it is more convenient to let the bird bathe inside the confines of the kitchen sink.

One of the prerequisites for bird bathing is that it should be simple and not too much of a nuisance or problem for the bird owner. If it is easy to bathe the bird, chances are that it will get done. Otherwise, there is procrastination of this necessary function.

Carrots Tops or other Greens in which a Bird would Dampen his Feathers

In their native Australia, parakeets will walk through the grass which is wet from dew. Greens may be moistened and placed on the floor of the cage. If this is convenient for the owner, it will serve as a twin function of giving the bird his bath and supplying him with his greens for his daily dietary needs.

Shower

The small sprinkler, like the type used for watering houseplants, can be used to shower the bird. Some of the larger birds will enjoy getting into the regular shower bath for people, and some have accepted being sprayed by the attachment on the kitchen sink. One young man who has several parakeets moistens a washcloth and wrings it out over his birds. He claims that it is about as simple and easy a method to shower a bird that there is.

Mist

Although probably not as natural as other types of bathing, a mist produced from a regular plant mister of the home garden variety, works well on a bird. The mist is allowed to settle down over the bird, as most birds don't like to be squirted.

Fountain

For those people who have an aviary or a cage large enough to support a small fountain, it is a luxury for a bird. The bird is able to splash around in the water, yet be rained on at the same time.

Food and Water Cups

Feeding dishes need to be manufactured from material that can withstand cleaning and disinfection.

In the average home, the dishes should be able to be placed in the family automatic dishwasher.

To have a double set of dishes would be a nice convenience, allowing extra time for cleaning.

Recreational Equipment

A cage would not be complete without some interesting toys or other playthings.

Swings

Standard swings are provided in most cages. A very interesting swing can be made from a string or rope. Loosely stretch the string from one side of the cage to the other, so the bird may rock to and fro, as a bird in the wild would land on a telephone wire.

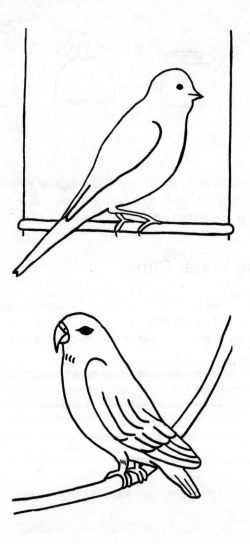

Peck Toys—Such As Dumbbells and Bounce Back

Toys that move or can be moved attract small birds. Owners will have to purchase several of these toys to find the best ones for their bird. These toys also intrigue large birds, but unless designed and built to be rugged, they will be quickly destroyed. Unused toys should not be left to clutter the cage.

Musical Toys—Bells and Musical Perches

Bells seem to be one of the most popular toys for small birds. When they peck at them, both the movement and the sounds hold their interest.

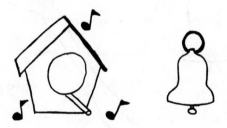

Reflection Toys

Mirrors, spoons, or any shiny object which might reflect an image fall into this category. The reflected image is assumed by your bird to be the friendly face of another bird. It is the kind of acquaintance that has all the qualities that one would like to see in himself—hospitable, non-aggressive, devoted, intimate. The bird may sit in front of the mirror for long periods of time with such enrapture that he will seemingly almost forget everything else.

More information on page 30.

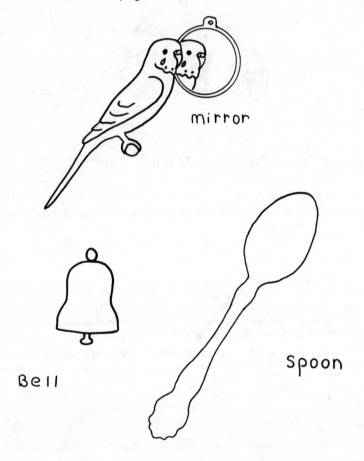

mirror

Bell

Spoon

Chew Toys Such as: Cork, Bones, Wood, Balls, Paper, Fresh Branches, Spools

Chewing is a natural quality in many birds. The curved beak of the psittacine family (all birds with a hooked bill) is meant for chewing.

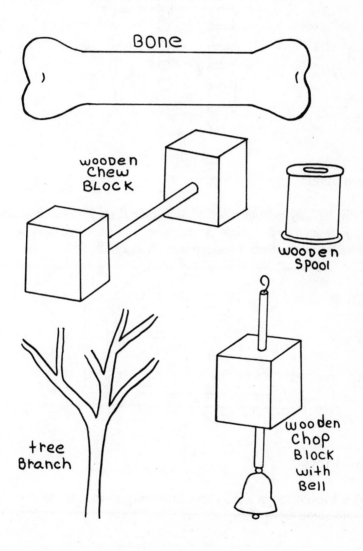

Bone

WOODEN Chew BLOCK

WOODEN Spool

tree Branch

wooDen Chop Block with Bell

Climbing Toys Such as: Ladders, Ropes, Chains

The rope or chain can be hung from the top of the cage and can be anchored or free swinging.

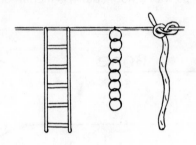

Playgrounds

Commercially manufactured or home-made playgrounds consisting of swings, ladders, balls, jungle gyms, monkey bars and shallow ponds are interesting for the birds if enough room is available.

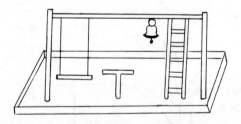

Action Toys

Good examples of action toys are merry-go-rounds, ferris wheels, elevators and rocking toys.

Hollow Tub Toys

Playthings of this type are home made from an empty can or carton and hung from the top of the cage.

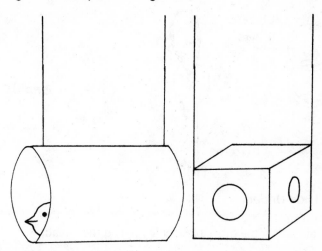

Bits and Pieces

Soft billed birds may enjoy emptying containers filled with paper balls or other paraphernalia.

Hanging Toys

Almost anything hung from the top of the cage might hold an interest for the bird. This includes bells, balls, boxes, keys, trapeze.

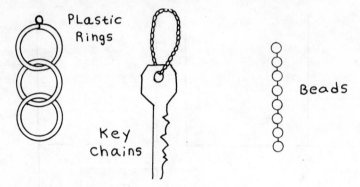

PLastic Rings

Key Chains

Beads

Toys to Hide Under

Parakeets and some other birds enjoy hiding their heads.

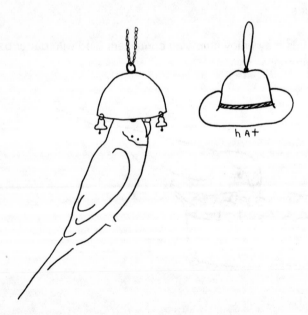

hAt

Puzzle Toys

The psittacine bird with its agile tongue and tremendous control of its beak enjoys unlocking cage doors, removing val clamps from homemade cages or key chains.

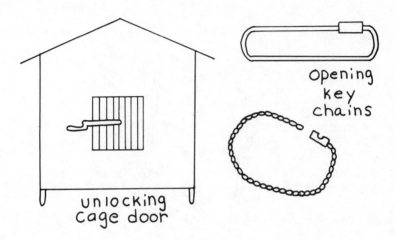

Opening key chains

unlocking cage door

Pull Out Toys

Plastic sticks inserted through a container can be removed by the bird.

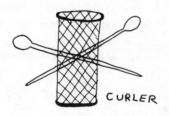

CURLER

Bead Toys

Beads hold a remarkable fascination for many birds.

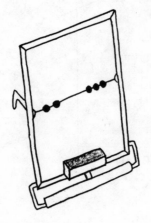

6 NUTRITION

Bird Owner's #1 Priority

> Many factors affect the health of birds; some we can control, some we can't. Fortunately, one of the most important criteria for health is within our control...diet.

Choosing the proper diet may be one of the most important decisions an owner has to make for his bird. Excellent health depends on an excellent diet. Birds in excellent health are spectacular to behold. So beautiful; so graceful; and remarkably adept at becoming a companion animal.

Pet bird owners generally have big expectations from their birds—love, companionship, entertainment, beauty, pride of ownership. Birds can accomplish these goals when they are well fed. Only with a high-quality balanced diet can excellent health and top performance be expected.

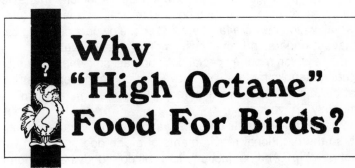

Why "High Octane" Food For Birds?

Although pet birds sit in cages most of the time, their metabolism and structure are those of flying machines. Even when not active, they have bodies with the capacity for tremendous and sustained exertion.

Their gift of flight and ability to perform extraordinary feats beyond the capablity of all other animals probably makes them the world's foremost super athletes.

Birds have survived and prospered through evolution because of their alertness, quick response to danger, and their ability to adjust to changes in the environment; all of which depend on internal speed (fast metabolism). A fast metabolism goes hand in hand with internal activities that generate heat. Warm bodies have been one of the birds' greatest assets. Without the benefit of internal heat, flight, itself, would be impossible. Day and night, birds' engines are hot and ready for action.

Flying machines require special fuel. No guesses—the fuel must be correct.

Speed consumes energy. This applies to cars, chemical reactions, as well as living things. Bird owners will be especially interested because birds have a fast metabolic rate—faster than the other animals with which they are familiar. Just as the owners of racing cars or airplanes understand that fast motors mean high operating temperatures which require special oils and gas, so owners learn that birds' "not metabolic motors" also have high operating temperatures, and that certain nutrients are required to keep their metabolism running smoothly.

Even as fuel requirements differ between the family car and the jet aircraft, so the nutritional requirements of a cat, dog or human vary from that of a bird. And not just any fuel will do. Foods have different caloric, protein, fat, vitamin and mineral values just as gasoline has various octane ratings. Selection of the proper foods is as important as choosing fuel for an aircraft.

Both, birds and aircraft, require high energy concentrated fuel. Birds, however, must digest, absorb and convert their fuel (food) into a useable form. Since food traverses the entire G.I. tract in 20 to 120 minutes, the process must take place rapidly and efficiently. The digestive tract is well-designed to accomplish this, but must be supplied with high quality digestible food low in fiber and cellulose.

Further, 40 separate nutrients make up the fuel needed to operate birds' engines. These ingredients must be renewed at each refueling (meal).

The dependency that birds have for fuel (food) places much emphasis on the role of proper nutrition in their life.

Nutrition is like a jigsaw puzzle. Only complete when all 40 nutrients are fed at each meal.

Ask Yourself

If you owned a valuable pet bird and wanted the bird to live a long, healthy, productive life, would you be concerned about his nutrition? What would you feed him?

Would you let a valuable bird randomly select the food he preferred from a variety of seeds and other food?

Are you sufficiently educated in bird nutrition to formulate or evaluate a diet?

Do you ever ask yourself, "What would be the best diet for my bird?"

> **IT MAKES GOOD SENSE TO FEED YOUR BIRD WELL. THE ONLY WAY HIS BODY CAN FUNCTION AT OPTIMUM LEVELS IS WITH ALL THE NUTRITION NEEDED DAILY.**

A balanced diet makes this relationship possible.

Commercial Diets are a Nutritional Bonanza for Pet Birds

With birds becoming more popular and valued pets, manufacturers have worked with avian nutritionists to develop better bird foods. The results have been gratifying.

Pet birds now can be assured the benefits of the best and latest advances. Owners no longer have to guess what variety of seeds and other foods might make up a complete diet.

Pet birds are the real recipients of these new efforts in bird foods. With excellent diets they can reach their full potential as pet and breeding birds.

To stay strong and healthy, every bird needs 40 nutrients in each meal.

Advantages of Commercial Diets for Pet Birds

Guaranteed Balanced Diets
The main benefit that manufactured diets offer bird owners is a balanced diet. The foods guarantee 100% of the nutrition needed for life and health.

Nutritional Integrity
High quality commercial diets have been formulated by leading avain nutritionists, and field-tested by knowledgeable veterinarians and aviculturists. Ongoing programs of evaluation and updating are used. Many products have an annual nutrition review so as to provide the finest in bird products.

91

Economy

Many steps and superior ingredients go into the production of high quality bird foods. These may initially cost more than other bird foods on the market, but a cost effective study will show you that, when waste is controlled, better bird foods can compete with the less expensive products. Since no vitamin, mineral or protein supplement need to be added, the total cost of the nutrition program is the cost of the food.

Further, the real economy of high quality bird foods is in the resulting health of the birds. Balanced diets offer birds a maximum opportunity for excellent health, longevity and a productive life.

> Why guess? Let avian nutritionists be responsible for your bird's nutrition.

Offers Unexpected Results

Many birds eating high quality manufactured diets have shown unexpected improvement in appearance and dispostion. No one really knows how well any bird can feel and act until they have been fed a guaranteed balanced diet. Birds are often judged to be in peak condition, but who really knows? The glowing reports of people who have changed their birds to a balanced diet confirm that many birds could be better than they are.

Birds are the world's foremost super athlete.

Controls Overeating

Birds eating a balanced diet will remain constantly at their normal weight, neither gaining or losing except for moderate seasonal fluctuations.

Changing Formulas
Since the appearance of the maintenance, and stress formulation pelleted foods varies only insignificantly, diets can be changed according to birds' nutritional needs without birds becoming alarmed about the change.

Quality Control
Laboratory tests are used to help keep food at formulated values and to assure users of a uniform product.

Variety Available in Commercial Diets

Cakes—Bars—Nuggets
A new type food for birds —AVI-CAKE FOOD— has been receiving much attention and rapidly becoming popular. Firmly compressed cakes, bars and nuggets offer an attraction to birds and their owners not found in other foods. This combination of seeds, pellets and natural flavors fulfills the balanced diet requirements and, also, makes birds excited about eating. The appearance attracts the birds, and once they start eating the flavor does the rest.

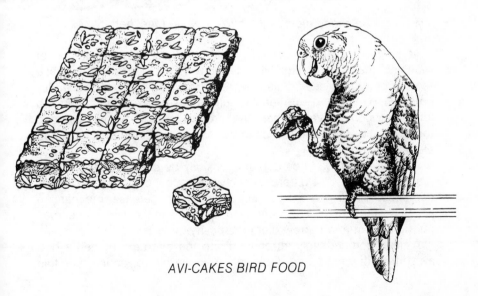

AVI-CAKES BIRD FOOD

These foods also provide the wonderful advantage of being a work and chew food as well as being nutritious. Birds revel in being busy, and these new foods make mealtime a "work and chew" occasion. When birds "work for their supper" they become more active, more spirited, and more responsive. In general, they seem to be happier and more satisfied animals. Being busy has a positive effect.

Pellets, Crumbles and Granules

Following the lead of successful nutritional achievements of other animals, bird seed manufacturers have marketed complete diets in the form of pellets, crumbles and granules.

Balanced diets make birds look and feel better.

Making a food into a pellet provides an economical method of reaching the goal of supplying birds with a balanced diet. While feeding other than seed diets is a break from tradition, it is needed for pet birds to reach the nutritional requirements for excellent health and long, productive lives. When the proper ingredients are blended together and formed into a pellet, birds are guaranteed a balanced diet in every bite.

Most seed eating birds can successfully be converted to pelleted foods, although some differences have been found in the speed of acceptance. Birds are suspicious animals—a defense mechanism which protects them from eating wrong things in the wild, sometimes restricts them to a narrow diet in captivity.

A new food suddenly introduced into the diet can frighten a bird away from his food, and, indirectly, deprive him of eating. For this reason, changing a bird from seeds to a pelleted food requires special attention.

Information on a number of methods to convert birds to pelleted food is available from Lafeber Comapny, RR# 2, Odell, IL 60460.

PELLETS ARE GENERALLY MANUFACTURED IN THESE FOUR SIZES—

LARGE PELLETS

Actual Size

MEDIUM PELLETS

Actual Size

SMALL PELLETS

Actual Size

CANARY PELLETS

Actual Size

Even though most pellets on the market appear similar, customers must depend upon the reputability of the manufacturer.

Diet Supplementation with Table Foods

That people should share some of their food with their pet bird seems natural. Sharing food can help <u>build a stronger bond between the bird and his owner</u> and can be a happy experience for the bird.

The question immediately arises as to which foods are harmful to birds. The answer is simple—birds can eat any wholesome food. Pet birds digest table foods well, so they can eat the same foods found on our table.

Your bird can eat any wholesome food.

Some precautions should be taken. Birds' gastro-intestinal tracts are designed to handle compact, concentrated foods such as—meats, fish, cheese, eggs, bakery goods, cereals, seeds, nuts, peanut butter and some vegetables like peas, beans, lentils, and potatoes.

Biting into a succulent food seems a delightful pleasure to a bird. The freshness and the flavor of greens and raw fruits and vegetables hold a special appeal. Many birds would prefer these as a large part of their daily diet and even "hold out" for these foods rather than eat their regular diets.

The moisture content of fresh greens and raw fruits is 75-95%. With water being the overwhelming component these foods are bulky. They also are especially low in proteins and calories. The combination of bulkiness and minor nutritional value suggests that these foods be only a small part of the total diet.

Another Precaution

Birds sometimes can develop habits similar to humans. A taste of some foods can delight them so much that they begin to enjoy eating just because they like the flavor. As you know, a diet based on taste appeal alone ends in tragedy.

Birds are best off eating 80% of their diet as a manufactured balanced food, and only 15-20% as treats, bakery goods, cereals, nuts, fruits, greens, vegetables, meat, fish or dairy products.

Washing Food

Fruits and vegetables should be washed before giving them to your bird. It only takes a small amount of insecticide, herbicide or fungicide to be toxic.

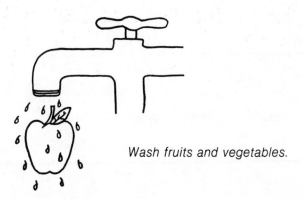

Wash fruits and vegetables.

Food Danger—Moldy Foods

Unexplained sickness and death in birds may likely be a result of food contaminated with the toxins from fungi. Mold growing on food under favorable environmental conditions can produce harmful compounds. Poisoning occurs when these foods are eaten. Birds may be one of the most susceptible animals to these noxious products.

Seeds in Birds' Diet

Seeds can be a good and important food in the diet of pet birds. As with any food, their use depends upon their nutritional value. Because of the enormous variations in nutrient content from one seed to another, and to avoid misuse of seeds, certain facts should be considered.

Seeds can be an excellent food for pet birds <u>when used as part of a total nutrition program.</u>

The nutritional value of seeds can well be compared to grains—oats, corn, wheat, etc. These are all excellent foods and have an important role in supplying the nutritional needs for humans. No one, though, would remain healthly living on just oats and corn, or some combination of grains. There is no single natural food that will fill all the dietary requirements for people or birds. Seeds, in general—like grains, are incomplete foods lacking in certain vitamins, minerals and proteins.

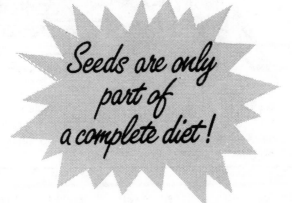

Seeds are only part of a complete diet!

If a diet is based on a certain variety of seeds and other foods, then all the food offered needs to be eaten at each meal. If only part is eaten, likely the nutritional value will be lacking. As with any foods for birds, each meal needs to be a balanced diet.

Birds will always eat seeds. It's more than just tradition. Birds like seeds and always seek them out. Nature seems to have taught them that when other foods are not available, to eat seeds. In times of drought, famine and winter weather, seeds are an important life-saving food. An exclusive dry seed diet can be thought of as a "hard-times" or "survival" diet, usually eaten by wild birds when other foods are not available. These may appear nutritious, but ordinarily lack many of the nutrients needed for life and health.

"Good times" diets are found in the wild during spring and summer. At this time of year nature's restaurant provides an abundance of foods that appeal to birds' appetites and provides balanced diets. Some of the foods that comprise nature's menu are: bugs, insects, spiders, caterpillars, worms, larva, fish, sea life, ripe fruits and vegetables, greens, grains, pollen, etc. These foods contain the nutrients needed for maintenance, reproduction, raising young and molting.

Placing a variety of seeds and other foods in a dish and expecting a bird to pick out a balanced diet creates problems. Birds have neither the instinct nor ability to choose a balanced diet from a cafeteria of foods.

Free choice feeding a loose mixture of seeds and other food encourages birds to become picky eaters. Birds will approach their food dish as if more concerned about what not to eat, rather than what they should eat. Picking and pecking, spilling out, sorting through and finally selecting food, make up their daily routine. This highly undesirable situation fosters nutritional deficiencies in addition to wasting food.

The future of seeds as a food for birds will probably be their incorporation into cakes, bars, nuggets and in mixes with pellets, crumbles and granules.

Did you know that fresh seeds found in your garden, backyard, or in a field can be added to your bird's diet?

Some of the common ones are: ryegrass, timothy, cockspur, plantain and dandelion.

The Danger of Foods with a High Fat Content

People feeding birds in the parrot family know how much birds enjoy eating sunflower seeds. (In fact, in many instances their preference for sunflower seeds has been so strong that they refuse to eat anything else.) Some people have suggested that sunflower seeds are addictive. While this is not true, it illustrates the tenacity of parrots not to give up their favorite food.

Sunflower seeds as the main ingredient part of the diet invites disease. While they can contribute to a balanced diet, alone they are a deficient food much too high in fat.

Extreme as it may sound, a parrot eating most of his diet as sunflower seeds, is equivalent to a person living mostly on a diet of peanuts.

sunflower seed kernels	47.3% fat
peanuts, raw	47.5% fat
safflower seed kernels	59.5% fat
peanut butter	50.6% fat

Sunflower seeds, peanuts, peanut butter, and safflower seeds are all high fat foods that need to be restricted to a small part of the diet.

Birds on high fat diets develop many of the same type diseases that people do—hardening of the arteries, fatty liver disease, and cholestoral plaques with narrowing the lumen of the arteries. Thus, bird owners must govern the type and amount of fat in birds' diets as much as they do their own.

Vitamins. Minerals, Grit

Vitamins

Vitamins are interesting "micro nutrients" found in food. Small as they may be, they are involved, however, in virtually all body functions. Without them, metabolism of protein, fats and carbohydrates could not take place. Vitamins are essential for the development, health, growth and maintenance of normal tissue. In essence, they are the promoters of good health. Birds require 13 vitamins none of which can be manufactured by the bird, and, therefore, must be obtained exclusively from the diet. The exceptions are Vitamin D, which may be synthesized by ultraviolet radiation from the sun, and niacin which may be made to some extent from tryptophan, an amino acid.

**VITAMINS ARE THE MINUTE CHEMICALS
INVOLVED IN VIRTUALLY ALL BODY FUNCTONS**

GROWTH

REPRODUCTION

VISION

BONE STRUCTURE

SKIN

RESPIRATORY SYSTEM

MUSCLE

CIRCULATORY SYSTEM

NERVOUS SYSTEM

GASTROINTESTINAL SYSTEM

RESISTANCE TO DISEASE

Because of the intensity of a bird's metabolism, vitamins are "used up" at a faster rate than in most other animals.

The 13 Essential Vitamins needed by pet birds in their diets are:

Vitamin A	Pantothenic Acid
Vitamin D3	Pyridoxine
Vitamin E	Folacin
Vitamin K	Choline
Thiamine	Biotin
Riboflavin	Vitamin B12
Niacin	

Birds manufacture their own vitamin C, so they do not need it in their diet. The other vitamins come from the food eaten daily. Pet birds being fed anything less than a certified balanced diet probably should have vitamins supplemented to their diet. Choose a vitamin preparation that will adequately protect your bird—such as one containing all 13 essential vitamins.

Purchase vitamins from your pet store or veterinarian and then follow the directions closely.

Vitamin products can be administered to birds in their drinking water or in their food.

In Water: Place the amount of powder or liquid in the water as directed by the manufacturer or your veterinarian. A fresh solution should be made daily.

In Food: When mixing vitamins into a food that will be completely eaten, a smaller amount can be used than with drinking water. In general, only ⅓ of the amount placed in the drinking water needs to be mixed in the food.

Warning: Vitamins or any other supplements sprinkled on the seed gradually sift to the bottom of the dish, or else are lost when the bird hulls his seed. The bird undoubtedly ingests some, but how much? Too little? Too much? At best, it's a guess.

Commercially balanced diets are now marketed that contain all the essential vitamins in adequate amounts. These diets do not have to be supplemented with additional vitamins.

For good health vitamins are needed daily.

Don't Overlook the Importance of Minerals

Gold may be the most important mineral to people, but the value of calcium and 12 other minerals far surpasses gold in the life of birds. Every one of the billions of cells in the bird's body requires minerals to survive. Besides their involvement in body chemistry, minerals form the basic component of the bone skeleton.

Calcuim and other minerals keep bones strong.

The skeleton of the superathlete bird is made up of thin, lightweight bones designed to rigid specifications. Any structural defect caused by shortages of minerals, allows fractures and other painful abnormalities to occur.

Readily overlooked, mineral deficiencies occur surprisingly often. Like other dietary nutrients, they too, must be supplied in the proper volume and ratio to each other; and under or over supplies can be harmful.

Those elements of most concern in pet bird nutrition are calcium, phosphorus, sodium, chlorine and potassium. The other eight elements are required in mirco-amounts and for that reason are named trace minerals.

Of particular importance are relatively large amounts of calcium and phosphorus in the diet. These minerals are required mainly for the formation and maintenance of the skeletal structures and in egg production.

Contrary to life in a cage, birds in the wild have few mineral deficiencies. Access to soil, ash, insects and other sources provide a convenient supply of minerals. In captivity, many pet birds are fed diets mainly of seeds, greens, fruits and vegetables. These foods are mineral deficient and birds need other foods or supplements as sources of minerals.

The mineral supplements most commonly used are—

from your pet store:
  cuttle bone
  mineral block
  oyster shells
  mineral mixtures

from your kitchen:
  milk
  chicken bones
  egg shells

These are placed in the cage and the bird chews or eats at them free choice. As with foods, birds have neither the instinct nor ability to pick the proper amounts of minerals from the group of preparations placed in front of them. In any evaluation, it is a "hit or miss" system that works, but is not dependable.

As with vitamins the best source of vitamins is a balanced diet. Birds that are eating commercially prepared diets will receive all the mineral requirements in their food.

Besides being a source for minerals these products are also used as chew toys by birds. The beak activities associated with chewing on cuttle bones, chicken bones, etc. are beneficial. Birds eating balanced diets will chew mineral supplements, but will not overeat on them.

Grit as Part of the Diet

Birds have a superior digestive system partially due to their gizzard. Non-existent in other animals, the gizzard has the power to crush and grind pieces of food into a smooth creamy paste. In this form food can be rapidly digested, thus allowing the bird to process relatively large volumes of food daily.

Grit aids the grinding process. The small pieces of sand, tiny pieces of rock or even granite provide the gizzard with "teeth" to help chew the food.

Nature tells birds just to swallow their food—their gizzard will chew it.

While not essential in pet birds who hull their seeds, or are on manufactured diets, nature seems to tell pet birds to keep some grit in their gizzard.

In chickens, it has been shown that the size and strength of the gizzard is related to the hardness of the food and the presence of grit. With a well-developed gizzard, a stronger, healthier and larger digestive system occurs. The feeding of grit to pet birds may have these same advantages.

Commercially, grit is sold in pet stores as sand, fine pieces of granite or in grit mineral mixtures.

Birds on deficient diets when trying to find nutrients lacking in their diet will often overeat grit. Excessive grit can irritate and even obstruct the gastro-intestinal tract.

Grit placed in a dish or sprinkled on the floor—to be eaten free choice—presents no problem to birds on balanced diets.

The Thirsty Bird

Pet birds' size and fast metabolic rate may confuse owners as to their requirements for life and health. For example, parakeets in the average home at 75° F will drink 2.5 to 5 ml. or one half to one teaspoon of water daily. This volume hardly drops the level of water in the dish and easily could be brushed aside as almost unimportant. However, if a comparison is made between a 1 ounce parakeet and a 150 pound human, the ½ teaspoonful of water would suddenly become approximately 10 gallons.

Provide fresh clean water daily.

Birds are thirsty animals, and in proportion to their size, require large volumes of water. Depriving birds of water is more dangerous to their health than a person would think.

Water

No life exists without water. The availability and quality of water influences to a large degree the vitality of life.

Being the largest single component of the body, water enters into almost all the body functions and acts as the main substance in the transportation of nutrients, chemicals, and waste to and from all the billions of body cells. It forms the common denominator to all life processes.

The Need for Fresh, Clean Water

For optimum growth, maintenance of health and efficiency of food utilization, a constant supply of pure water is required. The value of having clean, fresh, wholesome water available for birds should not be underestimated. Although not ordinarily considered a food, water must be recognized as one of the most important foods a body requires for life.

Survival in the wild has taught birds to be on constant vigil for anything that might endanger their life or health. Thus, any change in the color, transparency or flavor may cause them to be suspicious of their water and to avoid it. In effect, this deprives birds of water almost as though the water wasn't there or frightens birds sufficiently that only a minimum amount of water is consumed.

Be Careful
When adding anything to birds' water, a change in the taste or color may cause birds to stop drinking.

Additives

Medicines, tonics, and even some vitamins when added to the water can act as a major hindrance to normal water consumption. If anything is ever added to the drinking water, birds' water consumption needs to be measured.

The Value of Water

As compared in importance to other foods, a starving animal can burn up all of it's carbohydrates and fat, half of its body protein, and 40% of its body weight and still survive. However, the loss of 10% of the body water causes serious disorders, and 20% causes death.

When shortages of water occur, the body tries to conserve by excreting drier feces and less watery urine. The make-up of the kidney allows the bird to excrete solid urine, this being white crystals of uric acid. Owners will note this as the white portion of the droppings.

Water shortages discourage breeding, affect the general health, decrease food consumption and utilization, handicap the circulation of blood and other fluids, and, in general, create a hazardous situation.

Water Consumption Will Vary

When birds are supplied fresh water and are allowed to drink as much as they desire, the volume consumed will be noted to vary upon a wide range of environmental and psychological needs. Birds normally require increased amounts of water during exercise, courtship, egg laying, feeding their young, and in warm weather.

Conclusion

For the serious pet owner or breeder, the message seems clear—ample supplies of pure, wholesome water in a clean, protected and readily accessible container. Chlorine added to water by cities as a purifier will not harm birds.

Normal Weight—Overweight

An Interesting Story

Nature has taken special measures to control the number of calories birds ingest so that Weight Watchers won't get much business from birds. Overweight would jeopardize flight.

Three million years of evolutionary design went into designing an efficient flying animal, and nature won't allow a build-up of fat to sabotage her efforts. To become a flying machine, every extra piece of anatomy that was not necessary had to be jettisoned. Heavy solid bones were replaced with light hollow ones; teeth were discarded; million of skin glands were eliminated for one preening gland; the body had nine large air sacs incorporated into it; and even one ovary of the female was deleted.

With all this emphasis on lightness, an "efficient computer" was installed which would allow the bird to consume only the amounts of energy needed for normal body functions. Logically, overweight birds can not fly sufficiently well to survive the rigors of the wild.

No fat birds up here.

Birds' computers, then, signal hunger and calculate accurately the needs of the animals which vary depending upon size, activity, environmental temperature, growth and reproductive state, and also notify when these energy requirements are satisfied.

The volume of food eaten would depend upon its caloric content. A high caloric diet would satisfy birds' needs relatively fast and cause them to eat less, and a low caloric diet would not satisfy the caloric needs as easily and would cause birds to eat a greater volume of food. The system protects in both directions—it keeps birds from becoming obese and it also drives birds to eat to satisfy their caloric requirements.

When birds become adults, their bodies maintain the proper weight for flying their entire life, with only small seasonal fluctuations. In a sense, birds are guaranteed a prefect figure.

Well, how is it that some birds get fat? Although this statement may seem contradictory, about the only situation that allows birds to become fat is malnutrition.

To override the important weight control mechanism requires a serious problem, and when billions of body cells are missing certain nutrients, a craving develops which causes overeating. Birds crave for proper nutrition, and in their attempts to survive, they may overeat. The deficient body cannot rid itself of the extra calories and is forced to store them as fat.

Almost all fat birds can be considered suffering from malnutrition. Many of these birds also have fatty deposits in the liver, creating serious liver function problems.

Reducing fat birds, then, should be a matter of a diet correction. If these birds are changed to a balanced diet, the weight reduction will come automatically.

An exception to the rule of weight control in birds has been birds who have become so humanized that they "pig-out" just as people do. They eat people food, enjoy the taste and begin to eat like we do—from desire—not from hunger.

These birds also return to normal weight without a reducing diet when fed a commercial balanced diet food.

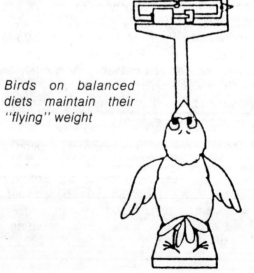

Birds on balanced diets maintain their "flying" weight

Mealtime Sould be a Special Occasion

Mealtime can be a rewarding experience for your birds when eaten in a relaxed and peaceful atmosphere. With the proper routine, the meal can be a happy event full of fun and enjoyment. Let each meal be a pleasant occasion, and at the same time an avenue for nurturing a loving relationship.

AN OCCASION FOR FRIENDSHIP, FUN AND GOOD FOOD

Challenging Tradition

The generally accepted concept of keeping food in front of birds all the time must first be challenged. Why do we do it? Tradition leads us to believe that birds might die if their dish isn't full all the time. But is this founded in fact? No! Food has probably been left in cages as a matter of convenience more than anything else. True, pet birds do need to eat daily, especially the small ones, but not continually all through the day.

Why then shouldn't we go along with tradition? The answer is simply... there's a better way.

Many of the answers we're seeking are found by looking into nature's design. "The goal of excellent health and peaceful existence for pet birds can be better reached when the footsteps of nature are followed." And what does nature do about mealtime?

If you examine the behavior patterns for all of the birds in the psittacine (parrot) family, you will find that nature has taught them primarily to eat two meals a day. And for good reason. By eating early in the day and again in the evening, they avoid exercise during the hot tropical day.

Daytime temperatures in the desert (home to the parakeets) and in the tropics (home to the rest of the psittacine family) easily exceed 100 degrees F. Nature knows that heat kills and that heat coupled with poor air circulation becomes more dangerous to birds; and if you add high humidity as in the jungles, the situation can become precarious. (Heat waves in this country threaten the lives of hundreds of thousands of chickens. Poultry people take great measures to protect their chickens against heat).

Heat can kill.

Pet birds have a body temperature much higher than humans, 104-109 degrees. If those body temperatures reach 110 degrees it could mean death. That's why birds never run a fever when they are sick, and it's also why heat can be dangerous to them.

Nature wants to restrict their physical activities during the hot time of the day. Therefore, for tropical birds mealtime and food gathering activities take place when it's the coolest—early in the morning and late afternoon.

To assure that birds would not have to eat constantly, nature gave them a food storage area termed a crop. They fill their crop in the morning to provide food throughout the day, and then fill it again in the evening for the overnight fast.

<u>Nature did not create a situation in which birds were to continually eat.</u> Nature lets birds develop a robust appetite and then they gather food. Food gathering is really their most important daily activity in the wild, and is a deeply instilled instinct. Hunting for food is carried on during their regular feeding hours or longer depending upon the availability of food. The only time birds fail this important task is when injured or sick.

To deny pet birds this task in captivity by having food constantly in their dishes can possibly initiate internal disorders. For harmonious living, birds need to daily "act out" the food gathering process.

While physically impossible for birds to actively hunt for their meals in captivity, it is possible for them to go through the food gathering process. This is reflected in their actions. They become more active during this period and also become more vocal and alert. The process goes on as if they were physically searching for food, and this activity, while mostly only mental, is to their advantage.

> **What actually happens when the birds are eating only in the morning and evening as in the wild?**
>
> The results will suprise you. You'll see increased activity, more alert attitutes and increased sounds. In other words—brighter, more responsive and active birds—happier birds. Besides psychological benefits, these birds also seem physically improved.

The Program—To Make Mealtime Exciting

Start by having food available for one hour in the morning and one hour in the evening. Initially, the food dish can be within the cage, but as time goes on, feeding outside the cage will be preferred.

When starting this program, birds may miss their first meal, but birds are smart animals, and at every other meal their crops will be filled. Even the tiny finch does well on two meals a day. The only birds not to feed in this manner are those that are sick or in their reproductive cycle.

Offer birds their food and then remove in one hour, or only give them enough food that it will be completely eaten in one hour.

When food is not available to be eaten, birds develop a normal appetite. The crop empties of solid food in about 6-9 hours, and then signals the birds to begin searching for food. In pet birds, if fed in the morning, food gathering would start in late afternoon. Even if the owner did not return until midnight, the birds would be in no danger of starvation or other physical harm as a result of not eating sooner.

Hunger is a sign that the birds' bodies are functioning normally, and is a signal that they should begin looking for their next meal. Hunger does not mean starvation. It is very comparable to another body signal—fatigue. Hunger tells us we should eat; fatigue tells us we should rest.

Hunger is an asset in another way also. As hunger becomes more pronounced, food looks better and better and an excitement builds as mealtime gets closer. Anticipation seems to stimulate.

Mealtime!

> Without hunger, mealtime would be dull, but with a keen appetite eating becomes enjoyable, and even plain food becomes tasty.

Added Enjoyment

Eating can mean even more than food to birds. If the owner takes time to hand feed or in some other way socialize with his birds, the human contact can mean as much to the birds mentally as the food does physically. Hungry birds consider the person bringing food a friend, and a bond of friendship gradually develops. Birds look forward to a relationship with other living things, and we, as owners, want birds to look forward to seeing us and wanting our friendship.

Mealtime, then, brings a joyful contact between birds and their owner.

Making New Friends

Food enters the picture again as the avenue to expand relationships to include more people and hopefully everyone. At mealtime or treat time people other than the owner should be encouraged to do the feeding. In time using appetite motivation, new friendships will emerge.

Mealtime, then, is an opportunity to make new friends.

Between Meal Snacks—Treat Time

Birds fed only at mealtime seem to be especially ready to accept a food treat.

They quickly learn that between meal snacks are fun, and besides, they like the extra attention.

Treats can include any of the quality products sold in pet stores, or any wholesome table foods. Birds seem to readily accept the food they see people eat.

Controlling Waste—Bird Owners Love It

When food is abundant, birds can waste tremendous amounts. They scoop it out of their dish; pick it up; chew on it; grind it up; tear it into pieces; play with it; sort through it; and eat only what pleases them.

What a contrast to birds being fed at mealtime in the morning and evening! These birds go through the mental food gathering process; anticipate mealtime, go to their food with a ravenous appetite, eat heartily and clean up all the food in the dish. No time for playing games. The birds concentrate on what they're supposed to do—eat.

A certain satisfaction comes from watching birds eat, and although an owner may at first feed just from duty, he will soon enjoy it.

The benefits gained from feeding a bird only at mealtime overcome any inconvenience.

Introducing Pet Birds to New Foods

Many owners are faced with the problem that their birds have developed bad eating habits. Trying to convert birds to eating a balanced diet is one of the most important concerns. This can be difficult.

Birds inherently resist change. They feel secure following a familiar routine. Thus, birds have an innate resistance to new foods.

Also, the suspicious nature of birds causes them to avoid any different or unusual food.

Fortunately, nature also designed methods to expand a bird's diet. Taking advantage of these will make the transition natural.

| OBSERVES | CONSIDERS | STUDIES | TESTS | FINALLY EATS |

Gradual Introduction of New Food

Birds normally alter their diet with the different seasons. Available food supplies gradually undergo a change. One food source diminishes and another becomes available. Even in nature birds are given time to adjust—no sudden change. Events take place gradually. This allows them to overcome their natural inhibitions through a process of observation, mental adjustment, and testing.

Procedure: Overlay the new foods with layers of seed or their usual food. The new food will slowly be accepted.

119

Young birds may convert to new foods in a week's time. Older birds and those that have been in small cages without much variety in their diet may take months.

Food Familiarity

Since pet birds are attracted to seed, a seed/pellet cake—AVI-CAKES BIRD FOOD—is a natural product to use when appealing to birds' visual senses. With the seed and pellets bonded together, birds eat the pellets when consuming the seed. For most birds, seed/pellet cakes are more than a balanced diet, they are an enjoyable and fun food.

AVI-CAKES BIRD FOOD

These seed/pellet cakes can be used as the sole balanced diet or as a halfway step in converting birds to a pelleted food.

Procedure   Break off one cube from the seed/pellet cakes (AVI-CAKE BIRD FOOD—Lafeber Company) and place it in the bird's feeding dish. When it has been chewed, replace with a fresh one. Repeat this until you are certain the bird has begun to eat the seed/pellet cake. Reduce the previous diet gradually and supply all the cubes that can be eaten.

Normal Hunger

Again, looking at nature's design, most birds in the wild eat mainly early in the morning and in the evening. Their morning hunger sends them searching for food until their crops are full, and their late afternoon hunger sends a message to fill their crops again. This routine protects birds from gathering food during the intense heat of the tropical day and gives them nourishment for the long overnight fast.

Duplicating nature's plan, feeding birds for a limited time in the morning and evening—and not in between—builds a hearty appetite.While in the wild, hunger motivates them to hunt for food; in captivity, appetite is the force which breaks the picky eater habits and causes them to seek new foods.

Procedure :   Feed your birds two meals a day—breakfast in the morning for at least 30-60 minutes—and then remove all of the food. Feed them supper in the evening for another 30-60 minutes or longer, and then remove all the food. At the same time, gradually begin introducing new foods.

Location for Feeding

Having meals outside of the cage has a positive influence on a bird's attitude on eating.

Try feeding your bird at least one meal a day outside of the cage.

Cages have certain negative effects on birds. Normal attitudes, adaptability, and curiosity become dulled. Anything new or strange can cause mental turmoil, fear, and nervousness. The longer they live within a cage, the more permanent are the psychological effects. Even an owner's hand coming into the cage with a fresh cup of food or water becomes a hostile intruder.

Birds leaving their cage to eat is the first step to opening up a whole new world. When birds eat outside their cage, it's like wild birds leaving a territory they've staked out in the breeding season. There can be a complete change in personality. They relax and become less defensive.

Eating outside of the cage allows pet birds to become more expansive and to regain their natural attitudes.

Procedure: In order to prevent birds from flying, the flight feathers can easily be properly trimmed by the veterinarian or pet store owner. Now the cage door can be opened and the bird encouraged to eat out of your hand or dish. When birds freely leave their cage, they generally climb to the top of the cage. It is a flat surface, and can be an excellent place to put the food and water dishes. The two meals a day program is used.

Peer Pressure

Experience has shown that pet stores and aviaries find it easier to convert birds to eating pellets than owners in homes. The presence of other birds seems to be a real force in helping birds broaden their appetite.

Procedure: Competition for food and group pressure prompt birds to eat new foods quickly. If one bird in a group eats pellets, then all may readily follow. Much of a bird's behavior is social conditioning. One bird's behavior depends in part on how other birds behave. The behavior of the leader is mimicked by the others. It is not surprising that groups of birds in flight cages will begin eating new foods readily.

7 ENVIRONMENT

Pet Birds' Surroundings

In a discussion of a bird's environment, consideration must be given to the cage, the surroundings, and all the activities in that area. The bird's house is his cage, but his home includes much more. For the bird to function properly and become an asset to his owner, he has to live in a pleasant environment.

Birds, probably more than any other animal, are sensitive to their surroundings. With suitable living conditions a bird will keep his feathers smooth and immaculately groomed—like a suit of clothes fresh from the dry cleaners.

Prepared or Unprepared for Cold and Drafts

Can it be that birds in the wild tolerate cold, wet, windy days, and that a bird in your home could become sick from a moderate draft? Seems contradictory, doesn't it?

One canary breeder, who has an outside unheated aviary, claims that occasionally in the wintertime he will have to knock the ice off the water before his birds can drink, yet his birds are tremendously healthy. This example is extreme, but is given to indicate that birds can tolerate moderate cold as long as they are healthy and well fed.

An incident that happened a number of years ago may give you an insight to a bird's ability to tolerate cold.

In December of that year a cold wave came down from the Great Lakes Region and when it hit Louisiana a large die-off of pigeons occurred. The deaths concerned the wild life people, until finally they declared that all the birds died from chilling.

Well, pigeons are the army tanks of the bird world. They are tough! The pigeons in Chicago had no problems with the sudden cold, and ordinarily the pigeons in Louisiana would not either. What happened?

The pigeons in Chicago had become acclimated to bad weather by their usual wet, cold, windy autumns. Louisiana had had an unusually warm, mild fall that year, and, thus, the pigeons were not prepared for the sudden cold.

Birds can acclimate themselves to pleasant or harsh weather conditions.

All birds have a built-in mechanism that allows them to tolerate harsh weather. These systems need to be "turned on" in order to function. The trigger to start the internal acclimating system actually is changes in temperature. When the need for it to function exists—it works, but when no need exists it "sleeps".

As seasons go through their gradual change, birds have ample time to prepare their heat regulatory system for what's ahead. The colder it becomes, the better prepared the body becomes for even worse weather.

The lesson to be learned from this "incident" is that birds can tolerate cold weather and drafts if their bodies are conditioned.

In modern homes the temperature fluctuates very little and birds are so well protected that their "furnace" rests. If temperatures suddenly drop - chilling easily occurs. The same thing happens with drafts because of the wind chill effect.

A draft of ten miles per hour at a temperature of 40 degrees has a wind chill factor of 28 degrees. Even a temperature drop of 10 degrees could be traumatic for a pet bird, and if that were accompanied by a draft, it could be sufficient to cause health problems.

In order to protect the birds in your home during the winter months drop the temperature in the bird's room at night. Gradually lower the temperatures from a few degrees to 5 to 10 degrees. The changes will not hurt your birds and will stimulate their heat regulatory system to handle drafts or colder weather.

Drafts will chill pet birds unless they have been acclimated to a wide range of temperatures.

Warning Signs

Unhealthy birds that look normal at 70° may show signs of their problems if the temperature declines slightly.

If the bird in your house is bothered by air conditioning in the summer time then move him to a warm room and consult your veterinarian. In general, birds tolerate cool temperatures better than hot.

Heat

Heat may be a bigger problem to some birds than the cold especially if coupled with high humidity. To keep from becoming overheated, birds need protection from the sun, good ventilation, and quiet. Birds left in the hot sun on a summer day will die from being overheated.

Humidity

An ideal humidity seems to be 40-50%, although a humidity much lower than this is well tolerated except in breeding conditions.

Clean Air

The spectacular, efficient respiratory system of the bird requires pure air flowing through the lungs, air sacs and sinuses. Unfortunately, nature didn't provide a filter designed to cope with all the modern air pollution. To contaminate this system with smoke, dust, and volatile chemicals leads to problems including death.

Any pollutant in the air can bother pet birds.

Cage Location

An area of family activity which provides the bird with the most socialization is probably the best place to keep him. In most homes the recreation room is the happiest place for the bird.

Outside walls, depending upon the temperature and amount of insulation, may cause undue exposure to cold. Drafts that are tolerated by us generally don't bother a bird.

127

The Lake Michigan waterfront in Chicago is especially beautiful. Mrs. Jones, who had a parakeet that had become particularly endeared to her, wanted her bird to enjoy the view. She had always lived several blocks from the lakefront and now had the opportunity to rent an apartment with a picture window facing the lake. Upon moving she carefully arranged the furniture so that the bird cage would be directly in front of the large picture window. Unfortunately, the bird could not tolerate the amount of light, and became psychologically and neurologically upset. After consultation with the doctor, he was put in a dark bedroom during the day. Even over a period of time the bird could not adjust to the picture window.

Animals, including people, become accustomed to a "status quo" routine and a very organized life. A variance from this can be upsetting and cause an internal turmoil which is reflected externally. How does this apply to birds? As strange as it may seem, a bird can become accustomed to living in one room or even become accustomed to the arrangement of the furniture. Changing things can fluster the bird. Most of the time they readjust quickly, and the temporary upset is not noticed by the owner. Of course, the bird not adapting must be moved back to his familiar surroundings.

In the organized order of things, birds can become used to being fed, having their paper changed, and receiving attention at a certain time of the day. When this varies, they can become upset.

As we are living close to a bird, and begin to have a feeling for him, we will learn to recognize these situations and help the bird through them.

Daylight and Darkness

Nature constructed birds to live within a balance of day and night. In fact, the influence of daylight and darkness has been so great that it has been said that birds are a "slave to light".

Many effects can be had by shortening and lengthening the amount of light that the bird receives in 24 hours. Poultry raisers for years have stimulated increased egg production by having the lights in their poultry houses remain on extra hours after sunset. For centuries the Japanese have forced caged birds to sing in midwinter by lengthening their days by using candlelight for three to four hours after sunset. Birds' migration is partially based on days becoming longer in the spring and shorter in the fall.

Pet birds probably require the same amount of light and dark that are occurring in a natural day. In the summer the birds would have eight hours of darkness daily and in the winter they would have about 12 hours of darkness daily.

Birds in the family recreation room that are kept up until midnight every night because of the television programs and who then have their sleep cut short in the morning because the sun rises early or light is turned on may be receiving only five to six hours of sleep every day. Inadequate amounts of rest for birds will cause constant stress and eventually will show the result of this strain in a breakdown of their health.

The periods of light and dark can be controlled in pet birds with a heavy cage cover.

Music and Other Sounds

Canaries that hear other canaries singing on a record or over the radio return the song in a lively manner. Cockatiels are known to enjoy the beat and the sound of music, and squawk and cluck as long as they hear it, and stop when the music stops. They seem to enjoy making sounds with the music and it is to be encouraged.

The sound of electric motors has a stimulating effect on many birds. When people run their vacuum, turn on an exhaust fan or even use an electric razor, they find that their bird may sing or talk more. The "song" of the motors has no harmful effect, and birds' enjoyment of the sounds speaks well of a good effect.

Hot Air Ducts

Hot air furnaces deliver air warmed to approximately 130°. Pet birds cannot tolerate this temperature and, if their cage is placed in front of a hot air duct, they will quickly die.

Even if your bird has been chilled and you want him warmed as quickly a possible, do not place him in front of a hot air duct.

129

8 FACTS and CARE: BEAK and NAILS

The Parrot's Incredible Beak

Impressive. YES! A pet bird's beak receives a lot of attention—and for good reason. Like the pointed end of a spear it looks threatening and dangerous. The beak intimidates not only natural enemies, but people as well.

Being positioned at the end of a long and flexible neck, birds can swivel their beak quickly in almost any direction. This agility works well for birds and allows them to use their beak for many purposes—and the main function is not as a weapon.

The Incredible Beak

Sensitive—Lightweight—
Grows Continuously—
Cuts—Grinds

Through a remarkable evolutionary divergence in design, the parrot family was given a beak which can be compared to a set of carpenter's tools (crow bar, wedge, spike, and vise) and a powerful group of muscles to work it. The pointed beak can be driven into or under hard objects, and then by wedging a lever action breaks apart materials. The upper and lower beaks combine to be a powerful vise capable of holding or crushing.

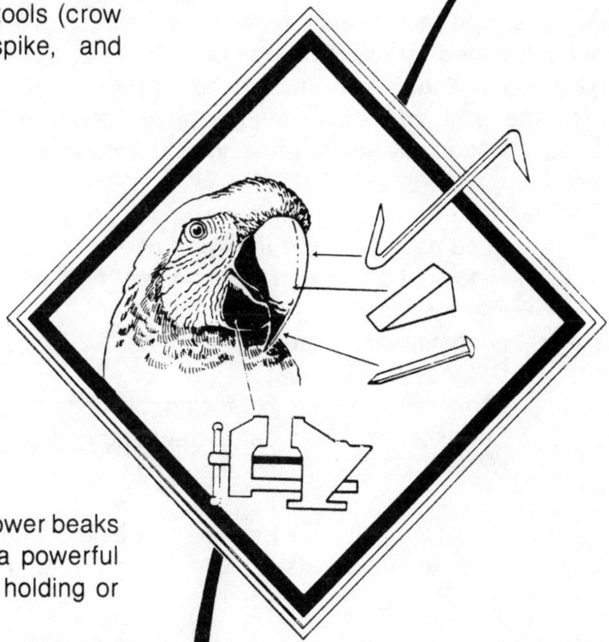

If you examined the underside of the hooked beak you would find that there are a series of ridges in a distinctive design somewhat resembling the surface of a craftsman's file. This irregular surface serves to hold any material pressed against it. Birds use these ridges when holding foods with their tongue and grinding them with their lower jaw.

The beak acts as a great set of carpenter's tools.

131

Crushes - Chops - Splits - Holds - Penetrates

In giving parrots an extraordinary beak, nature allows them to reach a supply of food unavailable to other birds. Much of the subtropical and tropical fruits, vegetables, nuts, and other food sources are protected by rough peels, rinds, horny coatings or hard shells. In addition, a variety of animal life hides under the bark of trees - in stumps of rotten logs, and in soil and decaying vegetation. To other birds, this wonderful food source is unavailable. Only a bird with special adaptations and ingenuity can reach these feasts.

Further, with the beak located at the end of a long and flexible neck, it has an added advantage of being highly maneuverable and accessible.

All these functions involve the beak:
Food gathering and transporting
Holding, hulling, picking, grinding
Pincers for getting into small areas
Grooming and preening
Defense and combat
Climbing, swinging, balancing, playing
Courtship, making nest and turning eggs, feeding the young
Noises - clattering and snapping

However, it is not all work for parrots. Being curious and fun loving, they want to know what is in, under, behind, and on top of most everything.

Structure of the Beak

It would be easy to surmise that the beak is composed of solid bone, and if you saw a parrot crack a large seed that would require a man with a hammer to open, you would be convinced. So strong and yet so lightweight, the beak functions as though it is solid bone and yet is hollow, except for fine, bony struts. The structure of the beak is well designed for birds' needs, but is not indestructible. When the beak is used for the purposes intended, such as cracking seed, removing the shell, and for other purposes listed, it serves birds well. BE AWARE! Unnatural forces applied to the beak may split and crack it.

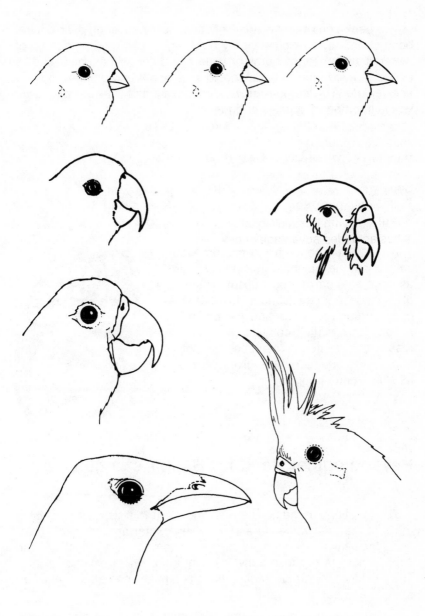

Normal beaks

The beak consists of a relatively thin, horny covering over a hard, bony structure. This outer horny covering or coreum is made up of material similar to the horns or antlers of other wild animals, and its normal appearance in birds should be smooth and uniform in color and texture. The coreum grows continuously, but the rate of growth varies in different species of birds.

Rate of Growth of Upper Beak (Approximate)

Canary	1⅓ to 1½" per year
Budgerigar (parakeet)	3" per year
Parrot	1¼" per year

If the tissue beneath the coreum were solid bone, the weight of the beak in a bird as large as a parrot could upset his sense of balance and equilibrium. Instead, the bony portion is porous and the center is hollow (pneumatic) connecting with the respiratory system. In spite of being porous, the bony structure gives the beak its shape and strength.

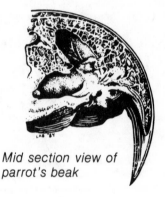

Mid section view of parrot's beak

Psychological Need for Beak Activities

The functions of the beak are so important to a parrot's survival in the wild that his whole life and activities center around them. Thus, using the beak for its intended purposes seems to be a "must", and to deprive parrots of these activities may affect them psychologically. The blocking of ingrained adaptations potentially can affect behavior, attitude and personality.

Experience and observation confirm that in captivity the bird who uses his beak for its designed purposes has a better chance of becoming a calm, personal pet. The beak's rapid growth confirms the amount of natural use it would have in the wild.

Chewing keeps birds happy.

Physical Need for Beak Activities

To maintain its shape the beak wears on the inside, outside and at the tip. In the normal eating process, food is picked up, held, rotated, and broken into pieces by grinding and crushing. These activities wear at the edges and inside layers of the beak. A certain amount of friction takes place from direct grinding between the tip of the lower beak and the inside of the upper beak. The outside surface and tip wear off from rubbing and abrasion when manipulating wood or other hard objects.

The interaction of the upper and lower beaks help keep the length normal. The lower beak wears off the upper beak, and at the same time, is being worn down. Anything that interferes with normal beak and mouth activity allows for overgrowth of beaks.

135

The Power of a Parrot's Beak

An average size parrot will take a rib-bone, chip away at it until he uncovers the marrow, and then eat it. They can take nuts and crack the shell with relative ease and eat the meat out of the center. Folks who have housed their bird in a not-too-well-constructed cage have witnessed a parrot bending bars, removing the clips that hinge the doors, and breaking the welds. Perches made from pine are easily split and are a toy for as short a time as 24 hours. These birds are not to be discouraged from chewing. But in fact, should be supplied with bones, branches from trees, pieces of wood upon which they can exercise and wear down the beak in a normal manner, in the way nature prescribed.

A parrot should be able to chew through a pine 1″ × 2″ perch in 2 weeks

Beware of Overgrown Beaks

An overgrown beak may be a warning sign that the bird's vitality has decreased due to an illness. Some of the hardest diseases to recognize are those which gradually develop, and the main sign of a problem is decreased activity. Birds are experts at hiding their problem, and slight clues are sometimes the only apparent things we have to judge their health.

Any time a beak overgrows, the cause should be established. The source of the problem could be minor, but even then a physical examination by a veterinarian and an evaluation of the situation is warranted.

Care to Prevent Beak Problems

In the explanations of the normal beak, emphasis was placed on its structure and rate of growth. If these facts are understood, along with an appreciation for the importance of the beak, the following recommendations should be logical. Of course, for birds to have a healthy beak requires a healthy body and a completely balanced diet. These are basic to any other consideration.

In order to stimulate and encourage birds to use their beaks an owner may provide the following:

perches of soft wood
  for parrots - white pine
  for cockatiels and parakeets - balsa wood

branches from shrubs and trees, pine cones, sugar cane

chew bars, cakes and other foods

cuttle bones, mineral blocks, oyster shells, egg shells,

climbing toys - chains, ropes, ladder, nets.

nuts to crack and hull

hard biscuits

bones

chew toys

lava rocks

A sugar pine block filled with an exciting food encourages beak activities

Observing and caring for your parrot's beak is an important factor in your total bird care. After all it's "more than just a beak".

Nail Trimming

No rule of thumb will solve the riddle of the proper amount to trim off a toe nail. Only experience can guide you. The quick on many nails (the fleshy core of the nail) reaches further toward the tip than might be expected. In order to avoid cutting deep into the quick, the nail should be trimmed off a small amount at a time. By this procedure if the quick happens to be cut, the bleeding would be minor.

It is better to trim the nails and cope with a bleeding problem than to let the nails overgrow.

Many bird owners have the ability to trim their bird's nails and clip the flight feathers, and thus, save the time and money for someone else doing it. However, the possible disadvantages should be considered.

*Many birds won't tolerate any procedure on their feet, even if painless.

*Restraining these birds creates a frightening situation that might destroy the relationship between the bird and his owner. Pet birds need to trust their owner. Owners need to avoid anything which might cause their bird to associate them directly with fear or pain. Consider having your pet store or veternarian trim your bird's nails.

Exercise For Wearing Down Nails

When birds have freedom to exercise as they desire their nails will ordinarily wear down to proper length.

Space to move about, then, becomes important in maintenance of normal nails. Large cages and exercise pens with wood accessories or other materials that have a surface conducive to keeping the nails short are ideal.

Time To See Your Veterinarian

A decrease in your bird's activity or a weakening of your bird's grip on the perch may be so gradual that it may not be apparent. These events, though, signaled by overgrowth of the nails may reflect a nutritional or medical problem.

When toe nails begin to overgrow, twist, or become deformed, see your veterinarian.

9 FACTS and CARE: EYE and EAR

Remarkable Eyes, Amazing Vision

The list of unusual and remarkable qualities of a bird includes colorful feathering, song, graceful nature, and flying ability; and yet, one of its most stunning attributes is its eyes. The eyes of a bird have reached the state of perfection superior to that of any other animal. This advanced state allows the bird to visually obtain more information about its surroundings than available to any other living thing. The eye collects data about the direction, distance, size, shape, color, three dimensional depth, and motion of an object. Whether this be an enemy or a food source, the bird has an advantage.

Exceptionally Keen Vision

Children attempting to "sneak up" on a bird are amazed that even though the bird is facing the opposite direction, their actions are detected and the bird flies away. The incredible range of vision is due to the placement of the eyes on the sides of the head. This fact, coupled with the shape of the cornea, allows for wide-angle vision. That a feather is one-fourth to one inch long.
not mean that he doesn't see it. Birds focus straight forward with both eyes, but also see sideways just as effectively. Their peripheral vision, especially related to a moving object, is also keen.

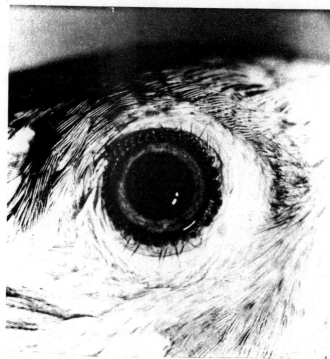

Birds' eyes may seem small but proportionately are much larger than ours. Note that the only visible portion of a bird's eye is the cornea. The largest part remains hidden. The eyelashes are small feathers—not hairs.

Birds have their vision fixed on you as soon as you enter the room, and you remain constantly under surveillance until you leave. Not that your bird necessarily mistrusts you, but they do have the ability to see you and everyone else present, even if the room is full of people.

You'll probably never be certain exactly what your bird's eyes are watching because their head does not point to the object under observation. And when your bird tilts his head he's just getting a look at you from another angle.

Predatory birds flying hundreds of feet above a field can detect a mouse with an ability unknown in other animals. With an extraordinary scanning and detection system, they can rapidly analyze the content of their field of vision and dive quickly on their prey. A person would take much longer to visually search the same space.

Skillful flight requires sharp eyesight and quick muscle coordination. An important part of flight is the bird's ability to focus rapidly. To avoid hitting branches when flying through trees and bushes or for catching insects in the air, birds have strong powers of near and far focusing.

Your bird has his "eye on you" when you are within visual range.

Adaptations For Superior Vision

To perform the functions nature has assigned, a large eye is required. For their size, birds have enormous eyes, although the mass stays hidden in the skull. The eyelids open to expose only that small part of the eye (cornea) needed to allow entrance of light. So while the eye externally appears small, the opposite condition exists.

Birds have three eyelids—an outer, upper and lower lid and the third eyelid just inside the others. The third eyelid (membrance nictatans) performs the job of cleaning and moistening the cornea. The inner surface is covered with cells which possess brushlike processes, so that the cornea is painted with tears at every blink. Like a windshield wiper, it cleans the undersurface of the eyelid on the return journey of each sweep. Pet birds blink with their eyelid 30 - 60 times a minute, and usually so swiftly as to be undetected. A large gland under the third eyelid furnishes much of the lubrication for the eye.

The upper and lower lid protects the eye and closes when the bird is sleeping. If the upper and lower lids are closed in a "sleepy" fashion, especially in an active environment, it can be a reliable sign of sickness.

> In summary, life as a flying animal demands superior vision.

Watching For Eye Problems

Birds' eyes are exceptionally resistant to some of the problems seen in mammals. Local infections, such as conjunctivitis, are unusual, but when troubles do appear, they are much more serious and difficult.

Because birds always want to present themselves as healthy, they face you with their good eye and hide an abnormal one. Thus, an eye infection may be missed until the owner becomes suspicious.

For any eye problem see your veterinarian.

Communicating Animals Require Good Hearing

Hearing is well-developed in all birds. The fact that they communicate by voice shows this. The way songbirds and parrots imitate sounds prove that they hear them the same way we do.

The bird's hearing covers about the same range as man's. It has been suggested that due to the broader construction of the hearing mechanism, birds are less sensitive to a wide range of sound frequencies than mammals, but more sensitive to differences in intensity. Further, a bird is able to hear and respond to rapid fluctuations in song about ten times as rapidly as man can.

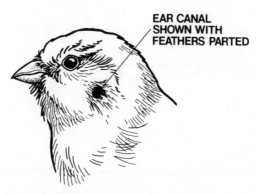

EAR CANAL
SHOWN WITH
FEATHERS PARTED

Feathers cover the ear canal.

The ear, besides its importance in hearing, is the organ of equilibrium. The basic structure of the inner ear reached such a high state of perfection, even in fishes, that its basic design has remained unchanged up the evolutionary ladder all the way to mammals.

The ear of a bird is not apparent because it has no external pinna (ear flap). Feathers hide the ear in all of our pet birds. To locate the ear, the feathers must be parted in the area below and in back of the eye. The ear at this point is merely a tube that carries sound waves from the surrounding air inward to the ear drum at its base. The wall of the outer ear canal may contain a number of small sebaceous glands. The ear glands secrete wax, but seldom is a buildup noticeable.

Recommendation: An infection, parasites, accumulation of wax or other abnormality would be signaled by a loss of feathers or the bird's rubbing the side of his head. These symptoms or any head tilt should be seen by your veterinarian.

10 FACTS and CARE: FEATHERS

An Engineering Marvel

The extraordinary gift of feathers has given birds a magic carpet which will sail virtually anywhere. This marvel of engineering design provides strong and flexible flight feathers that furnish the lift and thrust of flight whenever needed. With this flying ability, they have an effective monopoly on the sky—except for flying insects which are no competition for air space. Their freedom to fly where and whenever they desire grants them a free spirit unknown in other animals. Feeling secure in their ability to take quickly to the air, they are free to hunt and gather food adjacent to their natural enemies. No other animal makes its presence more conspicuous and with so much confidence as birds.

Soon after birth, birds are presented with expensive down-lined jackets that are carefully fitted to cover their entire bodies except for their feet and legs, and part of their faces. The down in these jackets is, likewise, guaranteed to keep the body warm in cold weather and is adjustable to keep the body comfortable in warm weather. This special coat has an outer covering of contour feathers that the designer has made beautiful as well as functional. When the wind blows, it serves as an excellent windbreaker; when it rains, the jacket is water proof. The thickness and strength of this coat protects the body thermally and mechanically. Besides all this, birds are given a magic carpet which is a marvel of engineering design. The flight feathers on the wings are strong and flexible, which give birds flight whenever they want it.

The key to water repellancy of feathers is the feather structure and feather network, not the natural oil. The micro-structure of the wide flat part of feathers involves interlocking barbules that may number up to one million in a single feather. The zipper effect gives strength to the web, but also traps air, helping to make the feather water tight.

In contrast to mammals needing a dull body covering to camouflage them from their enemies, flight has allowed birds to develop magnificent color and complex designs in their plumage. Whether the feathers are viewed from a distance or are scrutinized for their ultra detail, they can be thoroughly enjoyed by bird watchers, students, children and adults. Through all of history, men have marveled at the splendor of feathers and have attempted to duplicate their beauty. It seems fitting that birds as rulers of the sky have brilliant feathers to match their position.

Feather Facts

*   Feathers grow only in special patches or tracts, with intervening featherless spaces.

*   Feather coloring is the result of a combination of pigments and light refraction.

*   Lubrication of feathers decreases wear and is the function of the preening gland and powder down. (Powder down comes from a unique downy feather that grows continuously. The tips constantly disintegrate into a fine, talc-like powder. This powder helps waterproof, lubricate and preserve feathers. Powder down is obviously displayed in cockatiels and African Grey parrots.)

*   The preening gland at the base of the tail secretes an oil which the bird spreads with its beak onto its feathers and claws. In the pet bird class, some of the psittacines lack a preening gland.

*   The feather follicle normally begins to grow a new feather as soon as the quill of the old feather is removed. Within two weeks, the feather is one-fourth to one inch long.

* A bird's feathers must be replaced before they become worn out. The annual molt, replacing old feathers with new ones, is a dangerous time in a bird's life, since the expenditure of energy to replace its feathers leaves the bird vulnerable to illness.

* Complete feather care cannot be accomplished unless the bird is healthy both mentally and physically. Mental health demands companionship, a pleasant environment and security from stress. Physical health is related to a balanced diet, good sanitation and housing, and control of diseases.

Only birds have feathers.

Preening

Even the most fastidious persons don't spend as much time keeping themselves looking good as do birds. A good share of birds' waking hours are spent in preening. More than just good looks are at stake when it comes to feather care.

Feathers serve birds well, but they must be meticuously inspected, cleaned, lubricated and arranged at least once daily—and sometimes many times in a day. The task may take hours of work as average birds have more than 2000 feathers.

Nature's gift of flight demanded light weights, high power, and an aero-dynamically designed silhouette. Feathers are closely involved in all three.

First and most importantly, feathers must provide the insulation needed to maintain a hot body. To serve that purpose all feathers are cleaned of dust and dirt, and the down feathers are fluffed and un-tangled.

In the ritual of preening all the feathers are lubricated. Some birds use the oil from the preening gland near the base of the tail and others use the extremely fine powder down.

In either case feathers must be protected from wear. With only one set of feathers a year, and being in continuous use, if they become ragged and thin, they will lose their ability to carry out their functions. Birds seem to know that good feathering depends upon constant feather care, and so preen continually.

Preening is also a time for birds to check that each feather properly lies in its special location. To present an aerodynamically smooth surface each feather must fit the contour of the body.

At the same time the barbules coming off the main shaft are zip-pered together so that the vanes become a strong, wide, flat surface.

Feather Care Reflects Physical And Mental Health

Survival in captivity does not depend upon feather care as it does in the wild. Yet, for birds in captivity to be happy they need to continue performing these very important functions.

For pet birds to take excellent care of their feathers, everything in their lives needs to be "right". Feathers are the "report card" of how well birds are doing.

> Mental and physical health are the keys to excellent feathering.

Birds that have a "happy life" in captivity take excellent care of their feathers.

Nowhere is it more obvious that mental health depends upon physical health than in birds. With any sort of ailment or deficiency, birds become defensive and nervous. This in turn causes them to in-adequately groom themselves.

Encouraging Preening

Some pet birds either have never learned to preen, or their heritage for preening has been overshadowed by the stress of captivity. In any event, they can be helped. Preening can be stimulated through bathing and by encouraging beak activities.

Birds inevitably preen after being wet. So wetting their feathers daily will help.

Beak exercises promoted daily will encourage preening.

More information on page 137.

Bathing

Most pet birds enjoy bathing, and the ones that don't probably have never had the opportunity. If bird cages were made with shower stalls, all pet birds would participate regularly.

Bathing is fun.

Birds seem to know that water is good for their feathers, so wild ones sit in the rain when they could be under a shelter. Not always satisfied to have their outer feathers shed the rain, they will shift their feathers to allow the under feathers to become wet. Even on days when the temperature is in the 40's, cockatiels have been observed dancing in the rain until completely drenched, and enjoying it.

Owners can wet their birds' feathers in many ways:

*   Large birds can be showered in a bath tub or a regular shower.

*   In the summer any of the pet birds can be sprinkled with a fine spray from the garden hose.

*   Finger tamed birds can be sprayed in the kitchen sink or if spraying is offensive to them, wet with a small house-plant sprinkler—home-made rain.

*   Cockatiels and other birds of the parrot family may splash in a saucer if a mirror is placed on the bottom of the dish.

*   Canaries are always pleased with a saucer of water.

*   In Australia parakeets will bathe in grass wet with dew. A substitute for grass is wet carrot tops.

Comments: The temperature of water probably should be cool rather than warm.

Experience shows that good chewers are generally good preeners. Preening is a beak and tongue activity just as chewing—so any activity that stimulates chewing or other beak activities can also be beneficial for preening. The best preened birds are generally the best chewers.

Birds that are wet from the top shed water and remain dry. Birds sprayed from underneath become wet.

For birds that are poor preeners, wet their feathers daily, and promote beak activities with all the suggestions on page 137.

Birds like to shower frequently.

Molting—A Time For Special Care

In return for the many months' happiness that our birds give us, they need special care during molting. If people went through a molt or similar situation, we would appreciate the physical and mental stress. However, no comparable situation exists.

Molting is a primary factor in a bird's life. Nature has timed the molting cycle to occur under the most ideal conditions. Rarely does an event in the life of an animal occur where the environment becomes so involved with an internal process that intertwines nourishment, nutritional reserves, the endocrine (hormone) system, the circulatory system and the integumentary system. Nature provides warmth, rain, humidity, lengthening photoperiods, and a luxurious food supply. The bird must provide a good healthy body, have its reserves prepared, and its hormone system tuned to undertake a molt. The countdown starts when spring arrives. Molting in many birds starts after the reproductive cycle.

The birds of the parrot family don't generally have a complete molt, but molt periodically a number of feathers at a time.

Recommendations For Birds In A Molt

Heat—In normal molt, no area of the bird's body ever loses all its feathers. However, the feathering is definitely thin, and this may cause the bird to chill. To avoid this, the room temperature should not be allowed to drop.

Rest—Eight to twelve hours of total darkness per day will be required during the annual molt.

Security—Instincts direct birds to be quiet and stay hidden during an annual molt. The loss of feathers handicaps their flying skills which makes wild birds more susceptible to predators. The growth of hundreds of feathers also somewhat weakens them.

Pet birds feel the same stresses as wild birds. Birds start feather picking and other vices during a molt more than at any other time.

Providing birds with a quiet place, and covering part of the cage so that they have a place to hide reduces their anxieties.

Quiet—In nature, a molting bird resides in a peaceful, safe area . Molting pet birds should be kept in an area free of disturbances.

Preening—As the molting process begins, the bird becomes increasingly concerned with its plumage. When the quills begin to loosen, the bird removes them and is then ready to care for the new feathers. Each new feather is wrapped in a protective keratin casing. As the feather grows in length, its sheath must be removed before it can open. (The sheath is like a cover on an umbrella—the umbrella cannot be opened until the cover has been removed.) After the bird removes the protective coating the feather is still curled and the vein (flat part) is narrow. Preening flattens the feather and opens it to its full width.

With hundreds of new feathers regenerating, the bird must preen constantly. A white flaking material resulting from the bird's preening will collect on the cage paper and may alarm the owner, because it resembles heavy dandruff. Coupled with intense preening, it will cause some owners to think that the bird has dry, flaky, itchy skin. A natural but erroneous conclusion would be that oil is needed on the bird's skin and feathers. However, this powder is simply the residue of the keratin sheath, which the bird removes from around the feather, a normal and desirable process.

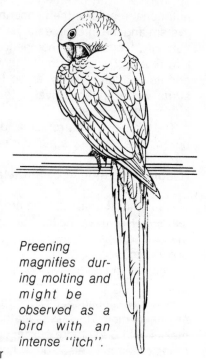

Preening magnifies during molting and might be observed as a bird with an intense "itch".

Balanced Diet—Molting is a test of the adequacy of the bird's nutritional state. Nutritional deficiencies are exposed probably more often during molting that at any other time of the bird's life.

Birds eating balanced diets should have no trouble satisfying their nutritional needs during a molt. However, to provide a margin of safety, birds are fed a diet with extra proteins, vitamins and minerals during this time—special need diets.

For birds not fed commercial balanced diets owners should add egg to their birds' food or other food with high quality protein.

Feather Picking

Why would a bird pick his own feathers out when he needs them for survival? The main function of feathers is not for flight but is to keep the body warm. Without complete feathering birds are susceptible to chilling.

Only birds with psychological problems would self-mutilate. They develop psychic behavior for a number of reasons—confinement, stress, fear, disease, parasitism, malnutrition, inactivity, boredom, etc.

The job of diagnosing the cause of these actions can be very difficult and sometimes impossible. If an effective treatment is to be had the cause needs identification. Even then, the treatment may be long. See your veterinarian.

Ruffled Feathers

Conserving body heat is the most important function of feathers. Whenever the body begins to chill, the feathers automatically respond by ruffling. The dead air space between the feathers increases according to the need. The greater the feathers thickness the better the insulation.

Birds will normally ruffle their feathers only when resting. Otherwise, ruffled feathers mean that something is wrong. Chilling may be caused by a cold environment or might come from within when the body doesn't manufacture sufficient heat because of sickness, loss of appetite or shortage of food. Birds with ruffled feathers should see their veterinarian immediately.

11 FACTS and CARE: RESPIRATORY SYSTEM

A Superior System

Nature built a unique respiratory system for birds to satisfy their rigorous demands for air. Volumes of air are needed to supply oxygen for their hot motors, and to keep their bodies from becoming overheated during periods of sustained muscular activity.

The avian respiratory system is the most intricate and efficient of any animal. Over millions of years a complex sophisticated system was modeled that could oxygenate the blood on both inspiration and expiration as needed for sustained flight over great distances, and for intense physical activities. Air constantly circulates through lungs that always stay expanded and communicate to large air sacs. The total volume of the respiratory system occupies up to 20% of the total body mass.

A System Worth Protecting

This large organ system is particularly susceptible to infection, and thus, requires added surveillance and care.

> Respiratory problems of pet birds are characterized by their slow, sneaky onset, and then their persistence to the point that the lives of the animals may be endangered.

Unlike typical respiratory problems of man (colds), which are self limiting and rarely are serious or have complications, the respiratory problems of pet birds must be considered potentially dangerous. If the initial respiratory infection doesn't kill the patient, there is a possiblity that the complications and after-effects will. The conclusion to be drawn from these statements is that the pet bird owner should be alert for the earliest signs of a problem, and then start treatment immediately. If respiratory diseases are not "put out" early, they can become deeply entrenched and difficult to treat. After these diseases become established, complications and after-effects occur.

Signs of Respiratory Problems

> The importance of maintaining a healthy respiratory system, and the need to recognize any slight abnormality immediately cannot be overemphazised.

Sneezing

Much information can be gained about the respiratory system by simply listening and watching. Unless you are an excellent observer and a keen listener, you probably have never heard a bird sneeze.

155

Sneezing is thought of in terms of our own experience. A person who is about to sneeze "winds up" with a deep inspiration, and then follows with a forceful noisy explosion of air out of the nose and mouth. Head movements and blinking of the eyes accompany this reflex.

comparative problems

Almost the opposite takes place with a sneezing bird. The sound produced would not attract any unusual attention. It could easily be overlooked as a normal sound, as it is soft and fast. In a room with moderate noise, it would never be heard. The bird's sneeze generates a sound somewhat similar to that of a noise made when a person snaps his moistened lips be gently blowing through them. Head movements and respiratory discharge are hardly detectable.

Sneezing occurs when there is an irritation deep in the nasal passage. It functions as a defense reflex mechanism to eliminate foreign material from the nose. The force of the sneeze aids in cleaning the nose.

Sneezing can always be considered a sign of a problem, and steps should be taken to remove the irritant, be it airborne or disease. Even though the sneeze of a bird is hardly noticeable, don't overlook this dependable sign.

Nasal Discharge

A discharge collecting in the nares, on the feathers above the nares, or on the beak is prime evidence of a respiratory infection.

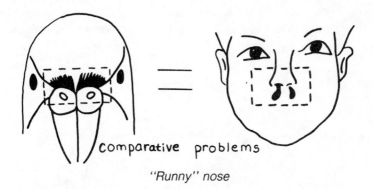

"Runny" nose

The feathers are stained dark due to a nasal discharge.

Coughing

Coughs in birds sound like "clicks," "chirping" and "clucks." It would be much better for the bird if the cough was loud and raucous. Attention would then be directed to the problem especially if the bird kept his owner awake all night due to the coughing. Just as with sneezes, it takes a trained ear to hear its occurrence. Always consider it serious.

comparative problems

Loss or Change of Voice

A canary that sings hoarse or off-key is just as abnormal as an out-of-tune piano. Generally, it isn't that the bird needs singing lessons or needs to be taught new lyrics. The problem is inflammation or infection.

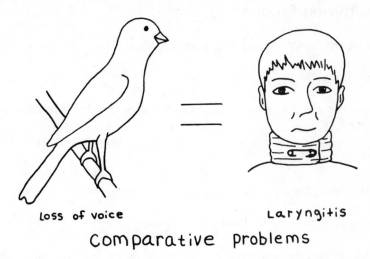

loss of voice   Laryngitis

comparative problems

Heavy Breathing

Respiratory sounds associated with increased or labored respiration probably reflect a *critical* condition.

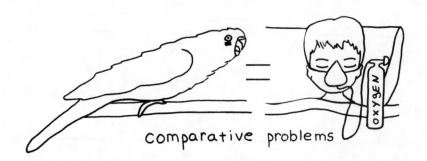

comparative problems

159

A description of other types of respiratory diseases and their complications would serve no purpose. The main thing to know is that they can happen, and if they do, consult a veterinarian immediately.

Recommendations

Besides the basics required for good health, it is most important to:

Prevent chilling.

Keep air clean—dust, dirt, pollutants are harmful to respiratory system.

Maintain humidity in air.

Keep nares clean.

Keep your bird isolated from other birds.

Seek veterinary assistance at the first indication of any respiratory system infection.

12 FACTS AND CARE: DIGESTIVE SYSTEM

A Super Efficient System

The design and function of the digestive system is based upon the bird's extraordinary need for nutrition and energy. The gastrointestinal tract is faced with the problem of transforming ingested food into a utilizable form of nourishment and energy for billions of cells. To visualize the size of the task, consider this example: a small bird may eat 25% of his weight in food daily. With a 20 gram canary (two-thirds of a ounce), that would be 5 grams of food. Not much volume in the palm of our hand, but compared proportionately to man, a 150 pound person would be eating 37 pounds of food. The question arises immediately of how a bird is capable of handling this volume of food? And futher, how could the digestive system begin to convert this bulk to a utilizable form fast enough to provide for the energy demands?

Refinement of the digestive system specifically for the purpose of processing proportionately large volumes of food is seen in the production line design of the gastrointestinal tract. The bird has two stomachs. The first one adds digestive juices to the food as it passes through on its way to the second stomach, which rapidly grinds the food into fine particles and sends it on to the small intestine.

By having a crop as the reservoir for food, it can deliver small amounts of ingesta continually to the stomach, where it can be rapidly processed. This makes for efficiency, as it enables a relatively constant process of digestion to take place. If the bird had teeth to perform these grinding

processes instead of the gizzard, the bird would spend a long time chewing its food, which would expose it to dangers that are avoided by its bolting the food down and flying to safety. Also, it is much more efficient to have the gizzard grind food for hours in a continuous action, as the quantity of food in proportion to the size of the animal is relatively great.

As food leaves the gizzard and passes into the intestines, it is mixed with digestive juices from the liver, pancreas, and the wall of the intestine. Bile from the liver acts to neutralize the acid from the stomach and to emulsify fats in preparation for further digestion. The pancreatic juices digest proteins, fats and carbohydrates. Once the food is digested, it is absorbed by the lining of the intestine, passed on into the blood stream, and distributed through the body.

The whole process must be synchronized and efficient, as the muscular activity of the intestinal tract propels the food through the intestine rapidly. A starling will have food pass through its digestive tract in twenty minutes, and in a parakeet, it takes less than two hours. The relatively small amount of feces in the droppings indicates the thoroughness of the whole digestive process.

The digestive system is functioning under this intensity because the bird has extraordinary demands for energy. Food, the fuel for the body, is burned at a much higher rate than for any other living thing. That this is true can easily be checked by noticing that the body temperature of pet birds ranges anywhere from 104^0 to 109^0.

Because energy is used rapidly, a bird must constantly depend upon food as a source of fuel. Fat reserves cannot be converted rapidly enough to energy to be of any importance. Any disturbance of the gastrointestinal tract which interferes with food digestion or absorption can cause the bird to starve to death in a few days.

The alimentary canal has many adaptions and unusual features compared to mammals. One of these, the cloaca, evolved to eliminate the need for a urinary bladder and colon. An exchange of an organ to replace two is good efficiency. To lighten the load—as needed in flight—the cloaca collects only a small volume and then empties, thus accounting for the many droppings which a bird has.

Since the cloaca has an influence on the arrangement and size of the droppings, knowing its structure makes interpretation of droppings easier. The feces enter from the large intestine on the bottom; the urine enters from the ureters (tubes leading from the kidneys) at the top. When the droppings are passed, the feces fall first, with the urine (white urates and fluid urine) coming second. In many cases, this allows the urine to cover the feces. A fold from the top of the cloaca separates the terminal part of the large intestine from the area where the urine is deposited. With this arrangement, at times urine is passed as a dropping without fecal material.

The oviduct (passage for eggs) enters the cloaca in the region of the ureters. When the female bird enters her reproductive cycle, the cloaca must enlarge to accept and pass the egg. The enlarged cloaca allows more material to collect, and thus, at this time the droppings become several times their regular size.

The capacity of the cloaca may vary from one bird to another of the same species. A 30 gram budgerigar may have 40-70 droppings daily, depending upon the cloaca size.

Passing Droppings

For purposes of insulation and warmth, feathers grow to the edge of the vent (opening for the passage of waste material). Thus, in the act of defecation, the feathers must be effectively parted. The bird raises his tail and combined with the increased tension of the abdominal muscles, the feathers divide. The action of the muscles of the cloaca, combined with the flicking of the tail, causes a temporary eversion and prevents any part of the elimination from adhering to the vent. This action is very rapid and the tail drops immediately.

Any time feathers are missing from around the vent or if the feathers in this area are soiled with feces, it can be concluded that the bird currently has or has had diarrhea.

Interpretation of Droppings

The bird owner has many good reasons to watch droppings daily. In fact, they are one of the best indicators of the bird's health.

Since birds effectively hide their sicknesses from our view, every means must be taken to recognize signs of sickness in pet birds. Because the droppings provide us with a wealth of information about the bird's health, it behooves us to watch them daily. A bird that develops diarrhea doesn't cause any mess in the house, nor is the diarrhea odoriferous. It is easy for the diarrhea to go unnoticed. If the dog had a similar diarrhea in the house, there is no doubt he would be taken to the veterinarian to have his problem corrected immediately. Likewise, if the dog started urinating in the house or started to wet the area where he slept at night, the owners would be disturbed and would have immediate veterinary care. The bird which is urinating more frequently than usual is fortunate to have his master even notice it. Urinary and intestinal problems could go on for weeks or months without the owner suspecting that something is wrong. Possibly the dog owner who takes his pet to the veterinarian for diarrhea may be more concerned about the mess in the house than the animal's health. With the bird, we don't even have a situation that irritates the household.

The bird depends upon a concerned owner and is much more dependent upon a giving master than the dog or cat is.

With reasonable awareness, information can be gleaned about the following:

Volume of Food Ingested

Because the bird's digestive system is short and efficient, the food which he eats today is passed through the intestinal tract today. Therefore, the fecal portion of the droppings reflects the quantity of food that he has eaten that specific day. The bird who fills his crop in the morning will pass feces all day even though eating no more until evening. The overnight droppings relate to the evening feeding.

A sick bird that consumes only half his regular volume of food will immediately decrease his droppings to half the normal volume. This same sick bird might be drinking an increased amount of water and thus passing more urine (white urates and water urine). Thus, there could be just as many droppings, but of urine content not fecal material.

Functioning of the Digestive System

The normal fecal elimination from the bowel has a green to black color, a finely granular texture, and carries the shape of the intestinal tract. Many factors have an influence on this description. Departure from the standard norm occurs primarily with the type of food in the diet.

Even when functioning normally, the feces will be eliminated in different colors, depending upon—the rate of passage through the intestinal tract, the type of food ingested, and the amount of water it contains. Bulky food, such as greens, passes through more rapidly and makes a green, soft stool. More concentrated foods make a drier, darker stool.

Problems of abnormal function may include:

Whole seeds passing in the droppings

The droppings becoming a light color
The feces changing to a coarser texture
Large bulky droppings

Other problems of abnormal function would require laboratory tests for their detection.

. In general, when the digestive system is not functioning properly, food is not being digested. The effect is the same as if the bird were not eating sufficient amounts of food. This, in effect, would cause an increased hunger and a weight loss. Some of these birds may be eating twice as much as usual and still be losing weight.

Abnormalities of the Intestinal Tract

Before attempting to evaluate droppings for abnormalities, a person should know normals. As a variation in size and consistency occurs between healthy birds, a normal should be established for each individual. This would best be done at the time the bird is purchased, as it will also serve to confirm the bird's health at that time. The stool has a range of shapes and colors according to the food ingested. In the course of 24 hours, some stools will be passed that appear unnatural, but the majority conform to the standard. This type of happening occurs and should not cause alarm. If the majority of the droppings lack their normal shape, an intestinal tract problem exists. The presence of irregular droppings warns of a problem but does not tell the cause of the problem. The following list of items should be considered:

INFECTIONS— virus, bacteria, yeast, fungus

PARASITES

DIET—moldy foods, decomposed foods, toxic foods, foods irritating to the intestinal tract

PROBLEMS THAT AFFECT OTHER PARTS OF THE BODY—may secondarily cause diarrhea: hepatitis, nephritis, pancreatitis

The following irregularities may be seen in the droppings of birds with intestinal tract problems:

RED BLOOD—Recent bleeding in the lower bowel.

BLACK BLOOD—Digested blood from the upper intestinal tract.

BROWN WATERY FECES—Severe infection—patient is critical.

MUCOUS COATING THE STOOL OR IN A LUMP ATTACHED TO THE END OF THE DROPPING—Indicates a chronic problem which may have existed for some time.

DARK GREEN BILE—The bird is not eating and is only passing bile. This patient is critical and needs immediate intensive care.

SOFT STOOLS WITH NO SHAPE—Diarrhea condition which needs diagnosis and proper treatment.

NO STOOLS AND NO BILE—Bird may be constipated or the intestinal tract blocked from some other problem.

HALF THE STOOL WITH NO SHAPE AND THE OTHER HALF WITH FORM—Diarrhea condition which needs proper diagnosis and treatment.

Droppings—As Involving the Urinary System

The kidneys serve a vital role in establishing and controlling the water balance of the body. The normal kidney, then, has the responsibility of maintaining the body at a rather static water level. In one 24-hour period, the kidneys could pass quantities of fluid urine and also pass very concentrated urine. The assumption could be made that these are normal kidneys. If they were abnormal, they would lose their ability to fluctuate between very concentrated urine and a very dilute urine.

Urine passes from the kidneys as white crystals of uric acid and as watery urine. Most birds pass both forms of urine under normal conditions. When water is in short supply, birds have the ability of conserving their own body water, and urinate solid urine as white uric acid crystals. When a bird drinks more or eats food with a high water content, he passes more watery urine.

Depending upon a bird's eating habits, some birds have a yellow pigment in their blood that is passed through the kidneys and is recognized in the dropping as yellow urates. These yellow colored urates may give some cause for concern, as about the same color develops if a bird is becoming jaundiced. If a person notices these yellow urates and the bird is not perfectly healthy, the bird should be examined by a veterinarian to determine if the bird has hepatitis.

Droppings and the Reproductive System

The cloaca of the female bird about to lay eggs will enlarge to be able to accept the egg from the vagina. The enlarged cloaca will be noticed by the size of the droppings that are passed. The droppings can become many times their normal size, but have every other characteristic of a normal dropping.

Should red blood be noted in the droppings, care should be taken in deciding if it is related to the intestinal tract, urinary tract, the cloaca, or possibly, the female system. In many cases, a retained egg in the uterus and vagina will cause bleeding. The important point to remember is that blood in the droppings can indicate trouble in other areas than the intestine and a proper diagnosis is hurriedly needed.

13 THIRTY-THREE DANGERS

In the course of everyday living sometimes we fail to notice the hazardous situations close at hand. Following are a list of potential dangers to your bird:

Transparent Window Glass

When allowed to free fly in your home, your bird will not recognize window glass and very likely will attempt to fly through it. Birds have been badly hurt and killed from such accidents. Initially, keep your curtains and draperies closed and then part them gradually as your bird becomes more familiar with the room.

Open Windows and Doors (Without a Screen)

In the summertime any number of birds escape from homes because of open windows and doors.

Mirrors

Mirrors have the same intrinsic dangers as transparent glass. Once your bird has become accustomed to mirrors in the room he will enjoy them as the bird on the other side will fascinate him.

Cats and Dogs

Most cats believe that small birds are fair game and will seek every opportunity to eat your canary, parakeet or finch. For the people who own a cat, the best suggestion is to obtain the cockatiel or larger parrot. An extremely vicious cat might attack these birds, but the average house cat won't touch them.

Over a period of time a dog can be trained not to bother a free flying bird. It pays to be precautious, and the bird should be introduced to the dog gradually.

People

The informed bird owner who takes care of his bird judiciously and seeks consultation early is truly the bird's best friend. More birds die from uninformed owners than probably any other reason.

Open Bowls and Pans of Water

Something seems to attract birds to water—possibly because it shines and glitters. Birds have been known to fly into pans of boiling water, bathtubs, toilet bowls, indoor swimming pools, etc. If your bird scalds himself, call your veterinarian immediately. Should he just get wet in a bowl of water, pat and dry him with a towel and keep him in a warm area until he is dry.

Open fish bowls are a hazard to pet birds.

Loud Noises

Birds enjoy many types of sounds and will be heard to sing and chatter along with them. Noises which begin to bother the human ear could also bother the bird. One parrot would pick his feathers out whenever the owners shouted at each other.

Fans

The danger of an open fan speaks for itself.

Inactivity

Beware of subtle signs of sickness. Birds hide their problems amazingly well. They can be seriously sick and show only decreased activity. These birds need prompt veterinary service.

Nesting Materials Made of Thread

Any cloth or material which will fray with threadlike ends serves as a real danger to the feet and legs of birds. The loose thread wrapped around the toes and feet, acts as a tourniquet. The thread will cut through the tissues with the potential loss of toes or feet.

Mange

Mange can be one of the causes of an abnormally shaped beak or lesions on the toes and feet. These problems should be looked into by a veterinarian.

Leg Bands

Breeders need identification on their baby birds. Aluminum bands are slipped over the toes onto the leg when the birds are only a few days old.

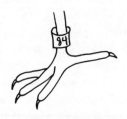

After the birds are sold, the leg band no longer has any purpose and should be removed. The two chief dangers of leg bands on a bird are: the band may catch on some object in the cage and cause the bird to fracture its leg; scales will build up under the leg band and act as a tourniquet on the leg. If the band stays on, the bird will lose its foot; if the band is removed, there is risk that the leg can be broken or that the blood vessels will be damaged and result in nicrosis (dry gangrene).

All leg bands should be removed from pet birds before problems develop.

Overheating

Most animals can tolerate cold much better than heat, and the bird is no exception. A bird left in the sunshine on a hot day with no chance to seek shelter will die from being overheated. Sick birds can be placed in incubators which may range anywhere from 85 to about 95° depending upon the seriousness of the problem and tolerate the heat very well. As these birds return to normal, the incubators become to warm for them and they draw their feathers very close to their bodies, holding their wings away from their bodies which helps eliminate the dead air space. At this point they will also be panting. When conditions such as thses are noticed on birds, it is time to get them to a cooler area.

Carbon Monoxide, Paint Fumes and Smoke

Any contaminant in the air is potentially harmful to a bird. School-teachers enjoy informing their classes that in the olden days, miners took birds into the mine shafts with them as a safety measure. The birds were quickly affected by poisonous gases. Their critical appearances would be a warning for the miners. The same can be true in private homes. There was an instance where a woman became hysterical because of the deaths one afternoon of her five birds. She telephoned the veterinarian frantically and was immediately warned to leave the house as poisonous gases were in the atmosphere. In fact, there had been a defect in her furnace which had allowed carbon monoxide to work its way into the forced air system in sufficient quantity to kill the birds and not yet affect the owner. Had the birds not died and she had stayed in the house, she, too, would have succumbed to the poisonous gas.

Burnt Teflon

Teflon coated pans, that are allowed to cook dry, can emit toxic fumes. A burnt teflon pan causes no danger to people, but birds will die from exposure to these fumes.

Poisonous Plants

A number of common house plants and garden ornamentals are toxic to birds if ingested. Ivy, poinsettia, and a species of dieffenbachia are included in a list of potentially dangerous plants listed in Current Veterinary Therapy.

Insecticides

Almost all insecticides are potentially poisonous to birds. Aerosols sprayed into the room to kill insects can also kill your bird.

PEST STRIPS—Are in the same class as insecticides.

Medicines

A person hardly realizes how many toxic materials are around until he starts handling birds. Medicines which seemingly are safe for people can kill birds. Be extremely careful in the administration of any drug; a bird is so tiny that overdoses of drugs are very easy—and overdoses can kill. As with yourself, handle medicines cautiously.

Antibiotics and other drugs sold in the pet shop for your bird should be used only when veterinary help is not available. Adding medicine to the drinking water can result in underdosages which will of course do your bird no good or may result in overdosages which might be toxic to your bird. Drug dosages must be calculated for the exact weight of the bird. This is the only safe way to use medicine.

FANCY MEDICINE cures everything

There are poor bird products on the market with deceiving names.

Wood Chips

Wood chips are sometimes used in the pans of large birds to absorb the droppings and as the method of keeping the cage clean. Particularly, young birds may get into these wood chips and eat them as food. Some very valuable baby macaws and cockatiels have died as a result of impaction following the eating of wood chips.

Vitamin B Deficiency

Vitamin B Complex is found mainly in the hull of the seed. If you have watched pet birds eat, they remove the hull from the seed thus leaving the part containing most of the vitamin B complex fall to the bottom of the cage. No wonder then that this is a commonly seen deficiency. Read the label on the vitamin product you are putting in the bird's drinking water to be sure that it contains the vitamin B complex vitamins.

Small Cages

One feels sorry for birds confined to a small cage. See page 62.

Toys

As with children, toys can be dangerous. Any sharp projection, wire, hook, or fiber could catch on the bird's feet or legs. Stay away from junk toys, and inspect closely anything you put in the bird's cage.

Long Toenails

If birds could talk, overgrown nails would be one of the most common complaints.

Overgrown Beaks

Overgrown beaks can create a serious problem for birds by interfering with normal eating.

Oil or Grease on feathers

Since the chief purpose of feathers is to keep the bird warm, anything that would damage or destroy the insulating power of feathers would be deleterious to the bird. Any oil or grease on the downy feathers will mat these feathers so that they cannot insulate the bird's body. Avoid using Vaseline, a commonly used preparation for areas of inflammation or irritation on people. It is probably in the medicine chest of every home in the United States.

The bird owner observes what appears to be an itching problem, concludes that there must be a problem with the skin in that area and applies oil or grease to help the bird's problem. The oil which had been applied to the skin is not satisfied to remain in one area and much like putting oil on the corner of a blotter gradually spreads to other areas affecting the insulation over a large portion of the bird's body. The bird will react to the insult by trying to remove the grease as best he can. He will seem to be picking and itching more but actually will be fighting for his survival. If the problem is minimal, the bird may overcome it. If there is sufficient grease on the skin and feathers, the bird will chill and die in a period of time.

Even small amounts of oil, grease, or "petroleum jelly" applied to the toes of legs can be troublesome. At times birds raise their legs to their body. This action spreads the oil onto their feathers. Whenever a bird's feathers look wet or pasted together from oil, it is a warning that there is a severe problem.

The *cardinal* rule is do not apply any oil or oily substance to the skin or feathers of a bird.

Cage Door Unsecure

Watch those cage doors! It is not unusual that birds escape from their cages through doors that are either left ajar or whose locking mechanism has become worn. The doors on about half of the cages (especially those of the bigger birds) are defective and need additional support to their locking mechanism.

Placing Birds Together in a Common Cage

Mixing birds can be dangerous for several reasons. They don't always get along together and can bite and pick viciously until the death of one of them. Also, one bird may dominate the other one until finally the bird is mentally affected, deteriorates and finally dies. Finally, one bird may reign over the seed cups and deny the other bird access to the food.

LEAD—IN PAINT, COLORED PICTURES, LABELS, FISHING WEIGHTS, LEADED LAMPS, DRAPERY WEIGHTS

These products may contain sufficient lead pigment to be toxic. Death from all these sources happens too frequently. Be careful.

Air Pollution

Whenever the news media broadcasts an ozone warning, include your bird as one of those animals which might be affected. Although not lethal, you might notice that your bird becomes inactive and seems stressed.

Hot Air Duct

Direct heat blowing on a bird from a hot forced air furnace can be fatal in a matter of hours.

Cage Decorations

Ribbons or any type fabric decorations used to decorate the cage (as at Christmas) are subject to being chewed and shredded. The threads entangle the bird or his limbs and can either trap him or act as tourniquets.

Val Clamps

Homemade cages for large psittacine birds sometimes have val clamps to attach the doors. Parrots may remove these and get them caught on their beaks. The mandible is not soild bone and can be broken. Clamps need to be removed carefully.

Botulism

Particularly a danger for outside birds, any bird eating rotten food or other decomposed organic material will die from this toxin.

Carpet

A bird picking or tearing fibers off pieces of carpeting and swallowing them can impact their crops.

For other dangers see Food Dangers on page 98.

14 SIGNS OF SICKNESS & EMERGENCY TREATMENT

CAN YOU JUDGE BIRDS' HEALTH BY THEIR APPEARANCE?

NO!

Critically Sick Bird.

Sick, Cold, and Hungry!!!

Birds are Masters at Hiding Signs of Sickness

LOOKING GOOD IN THE WILD— IT'S A MATTER OR SURVIVAL

Consider This- If you were a little bird in a whole flock of birds, and if you looked sickly, what do you think would happen to you?

Right, the flock would likely drive you off or kill you.

Now, under these conditions would smart birds ever look sick? No. They would hide any sign of sickness till they could no longer do it—and by that time they probably would be seriously sick or dying.

This is what happens in the wild, and is the reason why birds in captivity, also, cover up signs of sickness. They believe they're doing it for their own welfare.

Bird Owners Must be Particularily Alert to Detect any Signs of Sickness.

Otherwise, sickness can become well advanced before treatment is started.

If you talk to bird veterinarians, you'll find their universal plea is that sick birds be brought to them sooner. Their goals are to cure every patient, but they can't always do it when they are brought dying animals.

The question then for pet bird owners is: "What is ordinarily the first sign of sickness in birds?"

The Danger of an Appetite Loss

Birds' greatest asset (fast metabolism) can become their greatest liability when eating less than normal. Should the time come when anything happens that birds do not eat—be it a shortage of food, a lack of appetite from disease, injuries which prevent birds from getting to their food, or unfit food—there is an immediate effect upon the metabolism. Birds' bodies burn fuel so rapidly that lack of food quickly causes serious troubles. Shortage of nutrients causes the metabolic rate to falter, heat production to diminish, chilling and possibly shock. This unusual dependence upon a consistent source of fuel leaves birds immediately vulnerable when a shortage occurs.

Only bird owners who know how much their birds eat at each meal will recognize the first sign of sickness. Bird owners who keep dishes full of food rarely know how much or how often their birds eat. In some cases, birds can completely stop eating and the owner never realizes it.

Please read "Let's Celebrate Mealtime", pages 113 to 118.

Veterinarians treating birds at the first sign of illness have outstanding success. Everyone gains—the bird lives—and the owner is happy.

Signs of Sickness in Pet Birds

Appetite When birds develop sickness, besides being ill, they become nervous, defensive and fearful. In turn, their appetite and attitude toward food is affected. Understanding this, bird owners can detect important early signs that something is wrong by paying particularily close attention to their birds at mealtime.

Droppings Change in the character of the droppings or a decrease in the number or volume.

Activity Change in activity—generally observed as being less active, talking less, singing less, and overgrown beak and toenails.

Mood   Change in attitude, decline in friendliness—grouchiness.

Appearance Change in birds' appearance or posture. Ruffled feathers, eyes closing in a sleepy fashion, and sitting low on the perch (droopy)—are all serious signs of sickness.

Breathing Any noticeable breathing while resting, heavy breathing after exertion, change in character of voice, and any respiratory sounds—sneeze, wheeze or click.

Lumps   Any enlargement—even fat is abnormal in birds.

Lesions Unusual crustiness, discoloration or inflammation of face, beak, feet, or legs.

Bird owners will want to be watchful of their birds' health. Annual physical examinations are a good investment. Every new bird needs a complete physical. It's one of the most important examinations of his life.

Comparative Problems

A bird with ruffled feathers and partially closed eyes—is critically sick.

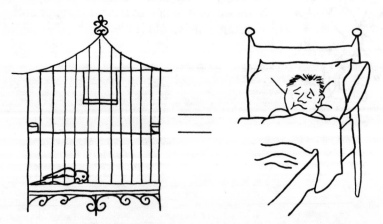

A bird lying on the bottom of a cage is probably dying.

Emergency Treatment

(Temporary Care Until the Bird Can be Seen by a Veterinarian)

If ever the bird sits with its feathers ruffled, eyes partially closed, droopy appearance, or if there are signs of diarrhea or respiratory problems, the bird should be treated immediately. Also, any bird which has been injured, sustained a broken leg or wing, bitten by a cat, dog or other animal, burned or chilled, should likewise be started on emergency care.

Every part of the following treatment is _important!_

Incubator

A temporary incubator can be made by placing a heating pad along side the cage and then the entire cage is wrapped with plastic and a cage cover. An infrared light or 150 watt light bulb could be used as an alternate heat source. The temperature should be maintained at 80–85°.

Should the cage temperature become too hot, the bird will start breathing rapidly, hold his wings out from the sides of his body, and the feathers will be held so close or tight to the body that he will appear peculiarly skinny.

Food

A bird that stops eating dies. Therefore, every effort must be made to encourage the bird to eat. Cups of food should be placed adjacent to where the bird is perched, or food scattered on the bottom of the cage if the bird is off his perch. The veterinarian will immediately force feed a bird by passing a stomach tube.

187

Rest

Sick birds need rest, and thus, should be in a darkened room or covered to insure 12 to 16 hours of sleep. A two-hour nap in the morning or afternoon is advisable.

Droppings

Start counting droppings. The number or volume of droppings will be of great concern to the veterinarian. Better yet, save the droppings for the veterinarian to view.

Don'ts

a. Don't give whiskey.
b. Don't use laxatives.
c. Don't use oil.
d. Don't stop food.

Telephone Your Veterinarian

Veterinarians hold the health of their patients, and the best interests of their owners as primary considerations.

INDEX